The Poetical Works Of William Collins

THE

POETICAL WORKS

OF

WILLIAM COLLINS.

WITH A MEMOIR.

vol 35

*Perennis
et
Fragrans.*

BOSTON:
LITTLE, BROWN, AND COMPANY.
1865.

rimus equis Oriens afflavit anhelis

Virg.

CONTENTS.

MEMOIR OF COLLINS.

"A Bard,
Who touched the tenderest notes of Pity's lyre."
HAYLEY.

No one can have reflected on the history of genius without being impressed with a melancholy feeling at the obscurity in which the lives of the poets of our country are, with few exceptions, involved. That they lived, and wrote, and died, comprises nearly all that is known of many, and, of others, the few facts which are preserved are often records of privations, or sufferings, or errors. The cause of the lamentable deficiency of materials for literary biography may, without difficulty, be explained. The lives of authors are seldom marked by events of an unusual character; and they rarely leave behind them the most interesting work a writer could compose, and which would embrace nearly all the important facts in his career, a "History of his Books," containing the motives which produced them, the various incidents respecting their progress, and a faithful account of the bitter disappointment, whether the object was fame or profit, or both, which, in most instances, is the result of his labours. Various motives deter men from writing such a volume; for, though quacks and charlatans readily become auto-biographers, and fill their prefaces with their personal concerns, real merit shrinks from such disgusting egotism, and, flying to the opposite extreme, leaves no authentic notice of their struggles, its hopes, or its disappointments. Nor is the history of writers to be expected from their contemporaries; because few will venture to anticipate the judgment of posterity, and mankind are usually so isolated in self, and so jealous of others, that neither time nor inclination admits of their becoming the Boswells of all those whose productions excite admiration.

If these remarks be true, surprise cannot be felt, though there is abundance of cause for regret, that little is known of a poet whose merits were not appreciated until after his decease: whose powers were destroyed by a distressing malady at a period of life when literary exertions begin to be rewarded and stimulated by popular applause.

For the facts contained in the following Memoir of Collins, the author is indebted to the researches of others, as his own, which were

very extensive, were rewarded by trifling disco-
veries. Dr. Johnson's Life is well known; but
the praise of collecting every particular which
industry and zeal could glean belongs to the
Rev. Alexander Dyce, the result of whose in-
quiries may be found in his notes to Johnson's
Memoir, prefixed to an edition of Collins's works
which he lately edited. Those notices are now,
for the first time, wove into a Memoir of Col-
lins; and in leaving it to another to erect a
fabric out of the materials which he has collected·
instead of being himself the architect, Mr. Dyce
has evinced a degree of modesty which those who
know him must greatly lament.

WILLIAM COLLINS was born at Chichester,
on the 25th of December, 1721, and was bap-
tized in the parish church of St. Peter the Great,
alias Subdeanery in that city, on the first of the
following January. He was the son of William
Collins, who was then the Mayor of Chichester,
where he exercised the trade of a hatter, and
lived in a respectable manner. His mother was
Elizabeth, the sister of a Colonel Martyn, to whose
bounty the poet was deeply indebted.

Being destined for the church, young Collins
was admitted a scholar of Winchester College on
the 19th of January, 1733, where he was edu-
cated by Dr. Burton; and in 1740 he stood first
on the list of scholars who were to be received at

New College. No vacancy, however, occurred, and the circumstance is said by Johnson to have been the original misfortune of his life. He became a commoner of Queen's,* whence, on the 29th of July, 1741, he was elected a demy of Magdalen College. During his stay at Queen's he was distinguished for genius and indolence, and the few exercises which he could be induced to write bear evident marks of both qualities. He continued at Oxford until he took his bachelor's degree, and then suddenly left the University, his motive, as he alleged, being that he missed a fellowship, for which he offered himself; but it has been assigned to his disgust at the dulness of a college life, and to his being involved in debt.

On arriving in London, which was either in 1743 or 1744, he became, says Johnson, "a literary adventurer, with many projects in his head and very little money in his pocket." Collins was not without some reputation as an author when he proposed to adopt the most uncertain and deplorable of all professions, that of literature, for a subsistence. Whilst at Winchester school he wrote his Eclogues, and had appeared before the public in some verses addressed to a lady weeping at her sister's marriage, which were printed in the Gentleman's Magazine, Oct. 1739, when Collins was in his eighteenth year. In January, 1742, he published his Eclogues, under the title of

* 21st March, 1740.

"Persian Eclogues;"* and, in December, 1743, his "Verses to Sir Thomas Hanmer on his Edition of Shakespeare," appeared. To neither did he affix his name, but the latter was said to be by "a Gentleman of Oxford."

From the time he settled in London, his mind was more occupied with literary projects than with steady application; nor had poesy, for which Nature peculiarly designed him, sufficient attractions to chain his wavering disposition. It is not certain whether his irresolution arose from the annoyance of importunate debtors, or from an original infirmity of mind, or from these causes united. A popular writer† has defended Collins from the charge of irresolution, on the ground that it was but "the vacillations of a mind broken and confounded;" and he urges, that "he had exercised too constantly the highest faculties of fiction, and precipitated himself into the dreariness of real life." But this explanation does not account for the want of steadiness which prevented Collins from accomplishing the objects he meditated. His mind was neither "broken nor confounded," nor had he experienced the bitter pangs of neglect, when with the buoyancy of hope, and a full confidence in his extraordinary powers, he threw himself on the town, at the age of twenty-

* Afterwards republished with the title of "Oriental Eclogues."

† D'Israeli, in his "Calamities of Authors," vol. ii. p. 201.

three, intending to live by the exercise of his talents; but his indecision was then as apparent as at any subsequent period, so that, in truth, the effect preceded the cause to which it has been assigned.

Mankind are becoming too much accustomed to witness splendid talents and great firmness of mind united in the same person to partake the mistaken sympathy which so many writers evince for the follies or vices of genius; nor will it much longer tolerate the opinion, that the possession of the finest imagination, or the highest poetic capacity, must necessarily be accompanied by eccentricity. It may, indeed, be difficult to convert a poetical temperament into a merchant, or to make the man who is destined to delight or astonish mankind by his conceptions, sit quietly over a ledger; but the transition from poetry to the composition of such works as Collins planned is by no means unnatural, and the abandonment of his views respecting them must, in justice to his memory, be attributed to a different cause.

The most probable reason is, that these works were mere speculations to raise money, and that the idea was not encouraged by the booksellers; but if, as Johnson, who knew Collins well, asserts, his character wanted decision and perseverance, these defects may have been constitutional, and were, perhaps, the germs of the disease which too soon ripened into the most frightful of human calamities. Endued with a morbid sensibility, which was as ill calculated to court popularity as to bear neglect; and wanting that stoical indifference to the opinions of the many, which ought to render those who are conscious of the value of their productions satisfied with the approbation of the few; Collins was too impatient of applause, and too anxious to attain perfection, to be a voluminous writer. To plan much rather than to execute any thing; to commence to-day an ode, tomorrow a tragedy, and to turn on the following morning to a different subject, was the chief occupation of his life for several years, during which time he destroyed the principal part of the little that he wrote. To a man nearly pennyless, such a life must be attended by privations and danger; and he was in the hands of bailiffs, possibly not for the first time, very shortly before he became independent by the death of his maternal uncle, Colonel Martyn. The result proved that his want of firmness and perseverance was natural, and did not arise from the uncertainty or narrowness of his fortune; for being rescued from imprisonment, on the credit of a translation of Aristotle's Poetics, which he engaged to furnish a publisher, a work, it may be presumed, peculiarly suited to his genius, he no sooner found himself in the possession of money by the death · of his relative, than he repaid the bookseller, and abandoned the translation for ever.

From the commencement of his career, Collins was, however, an object for sympathy instead of censure; and though few refuse their compassion to the confirmed lunatic, it is rare that the dreadful state of irresolution and misery, which sometimes exist for years before the fatal catastrophe, receives either pity or indulgence.

In 1747, Collins published his Odes, to the unrivaled splendour of a few of which he is alone indebted for his fame; but neither fame nor profit was the immediate result; and the author of the Ode on the Passions had little reason to expect, from its reception by the public, that it was destined to live as long as the passions themselves animate or distract the world.

It is uncertain at what time he undertook to publish a volume of Odes in conjunction with Joseph Warton, but the intention is placed beyond dispute by the following letter from Warton to his brother. It is without a date, but it must have been written before the publication of Collins's Odes in 1747, and before the appearance of Dodsley's Museum, as it is evident the Ode to a Lady on the Death of Colonel Ross, which was inserted in that work, was not then in print.

* June 7th, 1746.

" DEAR TOM,

" YOU will wonder to see my name in an advertisement next week, so I thought I would apprise you of it. The case was this. Collins met me in Surrey, at Guildford races, when I wrote out for him my odes, and he likewise communicated some of his to me; and being both in very high spirits, we took courage, resolved to join our forces, and to publish them immediately. I flatter myself that I shall lose no honor by this publication, because I believe these odes, as they now stand, are infinitely the best things I ever wrote. You will see a very pretty one of Collins's, on the Death of Colonel Ross before Tournay. It is addressed to a lady who was Ross's intimate acquaintance, and who, by the way, is Miss Bett Goddard. Collins is not to publish the odes unless he gets ten guineas for them. I returned from Milford last night, where I left Collins with my mother and sister, and he sets out to-day for London. I must now tell you, that I have sent him your imitation of Horace's Blandusian Fountain, to be printed amongst ours, and which you shall own or not, as you think proper. I would not have done this without your consent, but because I think it very poetically and correctly done, and will get you honour. You will let me know what the Oxford critics say.   Adieu, dear Tom,

" I am your most affectionate brother,

" J. WARTON."

Like so many of Collins's projects this was not executed; but the reason of its failure is unknown.

On the death of Thomson, in August, 1748, Collins wrote an ode to his memory, which is no less remarkable for its beauty as a composition, than for its pathetic tenderness as a memorial of a friend.

The Poet's pecuniary difficulties were removed in 1749, by the death of his· maternal uncle, Lieutenant-Colonel Edmund Martyn, who, after bequeathing ·legacies to some other relations, ordered the residue of his real and personal estate to be divided between his nephew William Collins, and his nieces Elizabeth and Anne Collins, and appointed the said Elizabeth his executrix, who proved her uncle's will on the 30th of May, 1749. Collins's share was, it is said, about two thousand pounds; and, as has been already observed, the money came most opportunely: a greater calamity even than poverty, however, shortly afterwards counterbalanced his good fortune; but the assertion of the writer in the Gentleman's Magazine, that his mental aberration arose from his having squandered this legacy, appears to be unfounded.

One, and but one, letter of Collins's has ever been printed; nor has a careful inquiry after others been successful. It is of peculiar interest, as it proves that he wrote an Ode on the Music of the Grecian Theatre, but which is unfortu-

nately lost.   The honour to which he alludes was
the setting his Ode on the Passions to music.

" TO DR. WILLIAM HAYES, PROFESSOR OF
MUSIC, OXFORD.

" SIR,

" MR. BLACKSTONE of Winchester some time
since informed me of the honour you had done
me at Oxford last summer; for which I return
you my sincere thanks.   I have another more
perfect copy of the ode ; which, had I known
your obliging design, I would have communicated
to you.   Inform me by a line, if you should
think one of my better judgment acceptable.   In
such case I could send you one written on a
nobler subject; and which, though I have been
persuaded to bring it forth in London, I think
more calculated for an audience in the university.
The subject is the Music of the Grecian Theatre;
in which I have, I hope naturally, introduced the
various characters with which the chorus was
concerned, as Œdipus, Medea, Electra, Orestes,
etc. etc.   The composition too is probably more
correct, as I have chosen the ancient tragedies
for my models, and only copied the most affect-
ing passages in them.

" In the mean time, you would greatly oblige
me by sending the score of the last.   If you can
get it written, I will readily answer the expense.

If you send it with a copy or two of the ode (as printed at Oxford) to Mr. Clarke, at Winchester, he will forward it to me here. I am, Sir,

"With great respect,
"Your obliged humble servant,

"WILLIAM COLLINS.

"Chichester, Sussex, November 8, 1750."

"P. S. Mr. Clarke past some days here while Mr. Worgan was with me; from whose friendship, I hope, he will receive some advantage."

Soon after this period, the disease which had long threatened to destroy Collins's intellects assumed a more decided character; but for some time the unhappy poet was the only person who was sensible of the approaching calamity. A visit to France was tried in vain; and when Johnson called upon him, on his return, an incident occurred which proves that Collins wisely sought for consolation against the coming wreck of his faculties, from a higher and more certain source than mere human aid. Johnson says, "he paid him a visit at Islington, where he was then waiting for his sister, whom he had directed to meet him: there was then nothing of disorder discernible in his mind by any but himself; but he had withdrawn from study, and travelled with no other book than an English Testament, such as children carry to the school : when his friend took it into his hand, out of curiosity to see what companion a man of letters had chosen, 'I have but one book,' said Collins, 'but that is the best.' "

To this circumstance Hayley beautifully alludes in his epitaph on him :

> He, " in reviving reason's lucid hours,
> Sought on *one* book his troubled mind to rest,
> And rightly deem'd the Book of God the best."

A journey to Bath proved as useless as the one to France ; and in 1754, he went to Oxford for change of air and amusement, where he stayed a month. It was on this occasion that a friend, whose account of him will be given at length, saw him in a distressing state of restraint under the walls of Merton College. From the paucity of information respecting Collins, the following letters are extremely valuable ; and though the statements are those of his friends, they may be received without suspicion of partiality, because they are free from the high colouring by which friendship sometimes perverts truth.

The first of the letters in question was printed in the Gentleman's Magazine :

" Jan. 20, 1781.

" MR. URBAN,

" WILLIAM COLLINS, the poet, I was intimately acquainted with, from the time that he came to reside at Oxford. He was the son of a trades-

2

man in the city of Chichester, I think a hatter;
and being sent very young to Winchester school,
was soon distinguished for his early proficiency,
and his turn for elegant composition. About the
year 1740, he came off from that seminary first
upon roll,* and was entered a commoner of
Queen's college. There, no vacancy offering for
New College, he remained a year or two, and
then was chosen demy of Magdalen college;
where, I think, he took a degree. As he brought
with him, for so the whole turn of his conversa-
tion discovered, too high an opinion of his school
acquisitions, and a sovereign contempt for all
academic studies and discipline, he never looked
with any complacency on his situation in the
university, but was always complaining of the
dulness of a college life. In short, he threw up
his demyship, and, going to London, commenced
a man of the town, spending his time in all the
dissipation of Ranelagh, Vauxhall, and the play-
houses; and was romantic enough to suppose
that his superior abilities would draw the atten-
tion of the great world, by means of whom he
was to make his fortune.

" In this pleasurable way of life he soon wasted
his little property, and a considerable legacy left
him by a maternal uncle, a colonel in the army,

* Mr. Joseph Warton, now Dr. Warton, head master of
Winton school, was at the same time second upon roll ; and
Mr. Mulso, now [1781] prebendary of the church of Winton,
third upon roll.

to whom the nephew made a visit in Flanders
during the war. While on his tour he wrote
several entertaining letters to his Oxford friends,
some of which I saw. In London I met him
often, and remember he lodged in a little house
with a Miss Bundy, at the corner of King's-
square-court, Soho, now a warehouse, for a long
time together. When poverty overtook him,
poor man, he had too much sensibility of temper
to bear with misfortunes, and so fell into a
most deplorable state of mind. How he got
down to Oxford, I do not know; but I myself saw
him under Merton wall, in a very affecting situa-
tion, struggling, and conveyed by force, in the
arms of two or three men, towards the parish of
St. Clement, in which was a house that took in
such unhappy objects: and I always understood,
that not long after he died in confinement; but
when, or where, or where he was buried, I never
knew.

"Thus was lost to the world this unfortunate
person, in the prime of life, without availing him-
self of fine abilities, which, properly improved,
must have raised him to the top of any profes-
sion, and have rendered him a blessing to his
friends, and an ornament to his country.

"Without books, or steadiness and resolution
to consult them if he had been possessed of any,
he was always planning schemes for elaborate
publications, which were carried no further than

the drawing up proposals for subscriptions, some of which were published; and in particular, as far as I remember, one for 'a History of the Darker Ages.'

"He was passionately fond of music; good-natured and affable; warm in his friendships, and visionary in his pursuits; and, as long as I knew him, very temperate in his eating and drinking. He was of moderate stature, of a light and clear complexion, with gray eyes, so very weak at times as hardly to bear a candle in the room; and often raising within him apprehensions of blindness.

"With an anecdote respecting him, while he was at Magdalen College, I shall close my letter. It happened one afternoon, at a tea visit, that several intelligent friends were assembled at his rooms to enjoy each other's conversation, when in comes a member of a certain college,* as re-markable at that time for his brutal disposition as for his good scholarship; who, though he met with a circle of the most peaceable people in the world, was determined to quarrel; and, though no man said a word, lifted up his foot and kicked the tea-table, and all its contents, to the other side of the room. Our poet, though of a warm temper, was so confounded at the unexpected downfall, and so astonished at the unmerited insult, that he took no notice of the aggressor,

---

* Hampton, the translator of Polybius.

but getting up from his chair calmly, he began picking up the slices of bread and butter, and the fragments of his china, repeating very mildly,

Invenias etiam disjecti membra poetæ.

"I am your very humble servant,

"V."

The next letter was found among the papers of Mr. William Hymers, of Queen's College, Oxford, who was preparing a new edition of the works of the poet for publication, when death prevented the completion of his design.

"Hill Street, Richmond in Surrey, July, 1788.

"SIR,

"YOUR favour of the 30th June I did not receive till yesterday. The person who has the care of my house in Bond Street, expecting me there every day, did not send it to Richmond, or I would have answered sooner. As you express a wish to know every particular, however trifling, relating to Mr. William Collins, I will endeavour, so far as can be done by a letter, to satisfy you. There are many little anecdotes, which tell well enough in conversation, but would be tiresome for you to read, or me to write, so. shall pass them over. I had formerly several scraps of his poetry, which were suddenly written on particular occasions. These I lent among our acquaintance, who were never civil enough to return them; and being then engaged in extensive business, I forgot to ask for them, and they are lost: all I have remaining of his are about twenty lines, which would require a little history to be understood, being written on trifling subjects. I have a few of his letters, the subjects of which are chiefly on business, but I think there are in them some flights, which strongly mark his character; for which reason I preserved them. There are so few of his intimates now living, that I believe I am the only one who can give a true account of his family and connexions. The principal part of what I write is from my own knowledge, or what I have heard from his nearest relations.

"His father was not the manufacturer of hats, but the vender. He lived in a genteel style at Chichester; and, I think, filled the office of mayor more than once; he was pompous in his manner; but, at his death, he left his affairs rather embarrassed. Colonel Martyn, his wife's brother, greatly assisted his family, and supported Mr. William Collins at the university, where he stood for a fellowship, which, to his great mortification, he lost, and which was his reason for quitting that place, at least that was his pretext. But he had other reasons: he was in arrears to his bookseller, his tailor, and other tradesmen. But, I believe, a desire to partake of the dissipation and gaiety of London was his principal motive. Colonel Martyn was at this time with his regiment; and Mr. Payne, a near relation, who had the management of the colonel's affairs, had likewise a commission to supply the Collinses with small sums of money. The colonel was the more sparing in this order, having suffered considerably by Alderman Collins, who had formerly been his agent, and, forgetting that his wife's brother's cash was not his own, had applied it to his own use. When Mr. William Collins came from the university, he called on his cousin Payne, gaily dressed, and with a feather in his hat; at which his relation expressed surprise, and told him his appearance was by no means that of a young man who had not a single guinea he could call his own. This gave him great offence; but remembering his sole dependence for subsistence was in the power of Mr. Payne, he concealed his resentment; yet could not refrain from speaking freely behind his back, and saying 'he thought him a d——d dull fellow;' though, indeed, this was an epithet he was pleased to bestow on every one who did not think as he would have them. His frequent demands for a supply obliged Mr. Payne to tell him he must pursue some other line of life, for he was sure Colonel Martyn would be displeased with him for having done so much. This resource being stopped, forced him to set about some work, of which his 'History of the Revival of Learning' was the first; and for

which he printed proposals (one of which I have),
and took the first subscription money from many
of his particular friends: the work was begun,
but soon stood still.   Both Dr. Johnson and
Mr. Langhorne are mistaken when they say, the
'Translation of Aristotle' was never begun: I
know the contrary, for some progress was made
in both, but most in the latter.   From the freedom
subsisting between us, we took the liberty of
saying anything to each other.   I one day re-
proached him with idleness; when, to convince
me my censure was unjust, he showed me many
sheets of his 'Translation of Aristotle,' which he
said he had so fully employed himself about, as
to prevent him calling on many of his friends so
frequently as he used to do.   Soon after this he
engaged with Mr. Manby, a bookseller on Lud-
gate Hill, to furnish him with some Lives for
the Biographia Britannica, which Manby was
then publishing.   He showed me some of the
lives in embryo; but I do not recollect that any
of them came to perfection.   To raise a present
subsistence he set about writing his odes; and,
having a general invitation to my house, he fre-
quently passed whole days there, which he em-
ployed in writing them, and as frequently burning
what he had written, after reading them to me:
many of them, which pleased me, I struggled to
preserve, but without effect; for, pretending he
would alter them, he got them from me, and

thrust them into the fire. He was an acceptable companion every where; and, among the gentlemen who loved him for a genius, I may reckon the Doctors Armstrong, Barrowby, and Hill, Messrs. Quin, Garrick, and Foote, who frequently took his opinion on their pieces before they were seen by the public. He was particularly noticed by the geniuses who frequented the Bedford and Slaughter's Coffee Houses. From his knowledge of Garrick he had the liberty of the scenes and green-room, where he made diverting observations on the vanity and false consequence of that class of people; and his manner of relating them to his particular friends was extremely entertaining. In this manner he lived, with and upon his friends, until the death of Colonel Martyn, who left what fortune he died possessed of unto him and his two sisters. I fear I cannot be certain as to dates, but believe he left the university in the year 43. Some circumstances I recollect, make me almost certain he was in London that year; but I will not be so certain of the time he died, which I did not hear of till long after it happened. When his health and faculties began to decline, he went to France, and after to Bath, in hope his health might be restored, but without success. I never saw him after his sister removed him from M'Donald's madhouse at Chelsea to Chichester, where he soon sunk into a deplorable state of idiotism, which, when I was told, shocked me exceedingly; and, even now, the remembrance of a man for whom I had a particular friendship, and in whose company I have passed so many pleasant happy hours, gives me a severe shock. Since it is in consequence of your own request, Sir, that I write this long farrago, I expect you will overlook all inaccuracies.   I am, Sir,

" Your very humble servant,

" JOHN RAGSDALE.

" Mr. William Hymers, Queen's College, Oxford."

The following communication, by Thomas Warton, was also found among the papers of Mr. Hymers.   A few passages, concerning various readings, are omitted.

"I often saw Collins in London in 1750. This was before his illness.   He then told me of his intended History of the Revival of Learning, and proposed a scheme of a review, to be called the Clarendon Review, and to be printed at the university press, under the conduct and authority of the university.   About Easter, the next year, I was in London; when, being given over, and supposed to be dying, he desired to see me, that he might take his last leave of me; but he grew better; and in the summer he sent me a letter on some private business, which I have now by me, · dated Chichester, June 9, 1751, written in a fine hand, and without the least symptom of a disordered or debilitated understanding. In 1754, he came to Oxford for change of air and amusement, where he stayed a month ; I saw him frequently, but he was so weak and low, that he could not bear conversation. Once he walked from his lodgings, opposite Christ Church, to Trinity College, but supported by his servant. The same year, in September, I and my brother visited him at Chichester, where he lived, in the cathedral cloisters, with his sister. The first day he was in high spirits at intervals, but exerted himself so much that he could not see us the second. Here he showed us an Ode to Mr. John Home, on his leaving England for Scotland, in the octave stanza, very long, and beginning,

Home, thou return'st from Thames.

I remember there was a beautiful description of the spectre of a man drowned in the night, or, in the language of the old Scotch superstitions, seized by the angry spirit of the waters, appearing to his wife with pale blue cheek, &c. Mr. Home has no copy of it. He also showed us another ode, of two or three four-lined stanzas, called the Bell of Arragon ; on a tradition that, anciently, just before the king of Spain died, the great bell of the cathedral of Sarragossa, in Arragon, tolled spontaneously. It began thus :

> The bell of Arragon, they say,
> Spontaneous speaks the fatal day.

Soon afterwards were these lines :

> Whatever dark aerial power,
> Commission'd, haunts the gloomy tower.

The last stanza consisted of a moral transition to
his own death and knell, which he called 'some
simpler bell.' I have seen all his odes already
published in his own handwriting; they had the
marks of repeated correction: he was perpetually
changing his epithets. Dr. Warton, my bro-
ther, has a few fragments of some other odes, but
too loose and imperfect for publication, yet con-
taining traces of high imagery.

"In illustration of what Dr. Johnson has re-
lated, that during his last malady he was a great
reader of the Bible, I am favoured with the fol-
lowing anecdote from the Reverend Mr. Shenton,
Vicar of St. Andrews, at Chichester, by whom
Collins was buried: 'Walking in my vicaral gar-
den one Sunday evening, during Collins's last
illness, I heard a female (the servant, I suppose)
reading the Bible in his chamber. Mr. Collins
had been accustomed to rave much, and make
great moanings; but while she was reading, or
rather attempting to read, he was not only silent
but attentive likewise, correcting her mistakes,
which indeed were very frequent, through the

whole of the twenty-seventh chapter of Genesis.'
I have just been informed, from undoubted au-
thority, that Collins had finished a Preliminary
Dissertation to be prefixed to his History of the
Restoration of Learning, and that it was written
with great judgment, precision, and knowledge of
the subject.

"T. W."

The overthrow of Collins's mind was too com-
plete for it to be restored by variety of scene or
the attentions of friendship.   Thomas Warton
describes him as being in a weak and low condi-
tion, and unable to bear conversation, when he
saw him at Oxford.   He was afterwards confined
in a house for the insane at Chelsea; but before
September, 1754, he was removed to Chiches-
ter, under the care of his sister, where he was
visited by the two Wartons.   At this time his
spirits temporarily rallied; and he adverted with
delight to literature, showing his guest the Ode
to Mr. Home on his leaving England for Scotland.
During Collins's illness Johnson was a frequent
inquirer after his health, and those inquiries were
made with a degree of feeling which, as he him-
self hints, may have partly arisen from the dread
he entertained lest he might be the victim of a
similar calamity.   The following extracts are
from letters addressed to Joseph Warton:

"March 8, 1754.

"But how little can we venture to exult in any intellectual powers or literary attainments, when we consider the condition of poor Collins. I knew him a few years ago, full of hopes and full of projects, versed in many languages, high in fancy, and strong in retention. This busy and forcible mind is now under the government of those who lately would not have been able to comprehend the least and most narrow of its designs. What do you hear of him? are there hopes of his recovery? or is he to pass the remainder of his life in misery and degradation? perhaps with complete consciousness of his calamity."

"December 24, 1754.

"Poor dear Collins! Let me know whether you think it would give him pleasure if I should write to him. I have often been near his state, and therefore have it in great commiseration."

"April 15, 1756.

"What becomes of poor dear Collins? I wrote him a letter which he never answered. I suppose writing is very troublesome to him. That man is no common loss. The moralists all talk of the uncertainty of fortune, and the transitoriness of beauty; but it is yet more dreadful to consider that the powers of the mind are equally liable to change, that understanding may make its appearance and depart, that it may blaze and expire."

In this state of mental darkness did Collins pass the last six or seven years of his existence, in the house now occupied by Mr. Mason, a bookseller in Chichester. His malady is described by Johnson as being, not so much an alienation of mind as a general laxity and feebleness of his vital, rather than his intellectual, powers; but his disorder seems, from other authorities, to have been of a more violent nature. As he was never married, he was indebted for protection and kindness to his youngest sister; and death, the only hope of the afflicted, came to his relief on the 12th of June, 1759, in the thirty-ninth year of his age, a period of life when the fervour of imagination is generally chastened without being subdued, and when all the mental powers are in their fullest vigour. He was buried in the church of St. Andrew, at Chichester, on the 15th of June; and the admiration of the public for his genius has been manifested by the erection of a monument by Flaxman, to his memory, in the Cathedral, which is thus described by Mr. Dallaway, the historian of Sussex:

"Collins is represented as sitting in a reclining posture, during a lucid interval of the

afflicting malady to which he was subject, with a
calm and benign aspect, as if seeking refuge
from his misfortunes in the consolations of the
gospel, which appears open on a table before
him, whilst his lyre and one of his best com-
positions lie neglected on the ground. Upon
the pediment of the table are placed two female
ideal figures in relief, representing love and pity,
entwined each in the arms of the other; the pro-
per emblems of the genius of his poetry." It
bears the following epitaph from the pen of
Hayley:

" Ye who the merits of the dead revere,
Who hold misfortune's sacred genius dear,
Regard this tomb, where Collins, hapless name,
Solicits kindness with a double claim.
Though nature gave him, and though science taught
The fire of fancy, and the reach of thought,
Severely doom'd to penury's extreme,
He pass'd in maddening pain life's feverish dream,
While rays of genius only served to show
The thickening horror, and exalt his woe.
Ye walls that echo'd to his frantic moan,
Guard the due records of this grateful stone ;
Strangers to him, enamour'd of his lays,
This fond memorial to his talents raise.
For this the ashes of a bard require,
Who touch'd the tenderest notes of pity's lyre ;
Who join'd pure faith to strong poetic powers ;
Who, in reviving reason's lucid hours,
Sought on one book his troubled mind to rest,
And rightly deem'd the book of God the best."

Collins's character has been portrayed by all

his biographers in very agreeable colours. He was amiable and virtuous, and was as much courted for his popular manners as for the charms of his conversation. The associate of Johnson, Armstrong, Hill, Garrick, Quin, Foote, the two Wartons, and Thomson, and the friend of several of these eminent men, he must have possessed many of the qualities by which they were distinguished; for though an adviser may be chosen from a very different class of persons, genius will only herd with genius. Johnson has honoured him by saying, that "his morals were pure and his opinions pious;" and though he hints that his habits were sometimes at variance with these characteristics, he assigns the aberration to the temptations of want, and the society into which poverty sometimes drives the best disposed persons, adding, that he "preserved the sources of action unpolluted, that his principles were never shaken, that his distinctions of right and wrong were never confounded, and that his faults had nothing of malignity or design, but proceeded from some unexpected pressure or casual temptation." A higher eulogium, from so rigid a moralist, could not be pronounced on a man whose life was, for many years, unsettled and perplexed; and those only who have experienced the pressure of pecuniary necessities can be aware of the difficulty of resisting meanness, or avoiding vice, if not in the sense in which these terms are usually understood, at least in a sense to which they may as properly be applied — that of refusing to prostitute talents to purposes foreign to the conviction and taste of their possessor.

On this mainly depend the annoyances and dangers of him who seeks a subsistence from his pen. The opinions which he may be desirous to express, or the subject he may be capable of illustrating, may not be popular, and the more important or learned they be, the more likely is such to be the case. Of course his labours would be rejected by publishers, who cannot buy what will not sell; hence no alternative remains but for him to manufacture marketable commodities; and when the *popular* taste of the present, as well as of former times, is remembered, the degradation to which a man of high intellect must often submit, when he neglects that for which nature and study peculiarly qualified him, for what is in general demand, may be easily conceived. It is not requisite to advert to the taste of the age in which we live, farther than to allude to the class of works which issues from the bazaars of *fashionable* publishers, and to ask, when such are alone in request, what would have been the fate, had they lived in our own times, of Johnson, Pope, Dryden, Addison, and the other ornaments of the golden age of literature? But if even in that age the Odes of Collins were too abstracted from mundane feelings, too rich in imagery, and too strongly marked by the fervour of inspiration to be generally appreciated, his chance of being so, by the public generally, is at this moment less; and the only hope of his obtaining that popularity to which he is unquestionably entitled, is by placing his works within the reach of all, and, more especially, by acquainting the multitude with the opinion entertained of him, by those whose judgments they have the sense to venerate, since they are sometimes willing to receive, on the credit of another, that which they have not themselves the discrimination or feeling to perceive.

An anecdote is related of Collins which, if true, proves that he felt the neglect with which his Odes were treated with the indignation natural to an enthusiastic temper. Having purchased the unsold copies of the first edition from the booksellers, he set fire to them with his own hand, as if to revenge himself on the apathy and ignorance of the public.

It is unnecessary to append to the Memoir of Collins many observations on the character of his poetry, because its peculiar beauties, and the qualities by which it is distinguished, are described with considerable force and eloquence by Sir Egerton Brydges, in the Essay prefixed to this edition. Campbell's remarks on the same subject cannot be forgotten; and other critics of the highest reputation have concurred in ascribing to Collins a conception and genius scarcely ex-

ceeded by any English poet. To say that Sir
Egerton Brydges's Essay exaggerates the merit
of some of his productions may produce the retort
which has been made to Johnson's criticism, that
he was too deficient in feeling to be capable of
appreciating the excellence of the pieces which
he censures. It is not, however, inconsistent
with a high respect for Collins, to ascribe every
possible praise to that unrivaled production, the
Ode to the Passions, to feel deeply the beauty,
the pathos, and the sublime conceptions of the
Odes to Evening, to Pity, to Simplicity, and a
few others, and yet to be sensible of the occa-
sional obscurity and imperfections of his imagery
in other pieces, to find it diffiult to discover the
meaning of some passages, to think the opening
of four of his odes which commence with the
common-place invocation of " O thou," and the
alliteration by which so many lines are disfigured,
blemishes too serious to be forgotten, unless the
judgment be drowned in the full tide of generous
and enthusiastic admiration of the great and ex-
traordinary beauties by which these faults are
more than redeemed.

That these defects are to be ascribed to haste
it would be uncandid to deny; but haste is no
apology for such faults in productions which
scarcely fill a hundred pages, and which their
author had ample opportunities to remove.

It may also be thought heterodoxy by the

band, which, if small in numbers, is distinguished
by taste, feeling, and genius, to concur in Collins's
opinion, when he expressed himself dissatisfied
with his Eclogues; for, though they are not without
merit, it is very doubtful if they would have lived,
even till this time, but for the Odes with which
they are published, notwithstanding the zeal of
Dr. Langhorne, who is in raptures over passages
the excellence of which is not very conspicuous.
To give a preference to the Verses to Sir Thomas
Hanmer, of which all that Langhorne could find
to say is, "that the versification is easy and
genteel, and the allusions always poetical," and
especially to the Ode addressed to Mr. Home,
on the superstition of the Highlands, over the
Eclogues, may possibly be deemed to betray a
corrupt taste, since it is an admission which is, it
is believed, made for the first time.   In that Ode,
among a hundred other beautiful verses, the fol-
lowing address to Tasso has seldom been sur-
passed:

"Prevailing Poet ! whose undoubting mind
Believed the magic wonders which he sung !
Hence, at each sound, imagination glows !
Hence, at each picture, vivid life starts here !
Hence, his warm lay with softest sweetness flows !
Melting it flows, pure, murmuring, strong, and clear,
And fills the impassion'd heart, and wins the harmonious ear ! "

The picture of the swain drowned in a fen, and
the grief of his widow, possessing every charm

which simplicity and tenderness can bestow, and give to that Ode claims to admiration which, if admitted, have been hitherto conceded in silence.

From the coincidence between Collins's love of, and addresses to, Music, his residence at Oxford, and from internal evidence, Some Verses on Our Late Taste in Music, which appeared in the Gentleman's Magazine for 1740, and there said to be "by a Gentleman of Oxford," are printed in this edition of Collins's works, not, however, as positively his, but as being so likely to be written by him, as to justify their being brought to the notice of his readers.

A poet, and not to have felt the tender passion, would be a creature which the world has never yet seen. It is said that Collins was extremely fond of a young lady who was born the day before him, and who did not return his affection; and that, punning upon his misfortune, he observed, "he came into the world a day after the fair." The lady is supposed to have been Miss Elizabeth Goddard, the intended bride of Colonel Ross, to whom he addressed his beautiful Ode on the death of that Officer at the battle of Fontenoy, at which time she was on a visit to the family of the Earl of Tankerville, who then resided at Up-Park, near Chichester, a place that overlooks the little village of Harting, mentioned in the Ode.

Collins's person was of the middle size and well formed; of a light complexion, with gray, weak eyes. His mind was deeply imbued with classical literature, and he understood the Italian, French, and Spanish languages. He was well read, and was particularly conversant with early English writers, and to an ardent love of literature he united, as is manifest from many of his pieces, a passionate devotion to Music, that

" ―――― Sphere-descended maid,
Friend of Pleasure, Wisdom's aid."

His family, which were very respectable, were established at Chichester in the sixteenth century as tradesmen of the higher order, and his immediate ancestor was mayor of that city in 1619:*

* Dallaway's Sussex, vol. i. p. 185 — The arms of the family of Collins are there said to have been, "Azure a griffin segreant or ;" but in Sir William Burrell's MS. Collections for a History of Sussex, in the British Museum, the field is described as being vert. From those manuscripts which are marked "Additional MSS." Nos. 5697 to 5699, the following notices of the Poet's family have been extracted.

REGISTER OF ST. ANDREW'S, CHICHESTER.

BAPTISM.

Elizabeth, daughter of Mr. George Collins, 8th October, 1768.

BURIALS.

Mrs. Elizabeth Collins [the poet's mother], 6th July, 1744.
William Collins, Gent. [the Poet], 15th June, 1759.

REGISTER OF ST. PETER THE GREAT,
CHICHESTER.

BAPTISMS.

Charles, son of Roger Collins, 8th February, 1645.
George, son of Mr. George Collins, 28th December, 1647.
Humphrey, son of Mr. Richard Collins, 20th Dec. 1648.

his mother's relations appear to have been of a superior condition in life.* Collins lost his father in 1734, and on the 5th of July, 1744, his mother

George, son of Mr. George Collins, 7th September, 1651.
Christian, daughter of Mr. Richard Collins, 1st Sept. 1652.
John, son of Mr. Richard Collins, senior, 13th Dec. 1652.
Elizabeth, daughter of Mr. Richard Collins, sen. 16th May, 1656.
Joan, daughter of Mr. Richard Collins, jun. 12th Dec. 1656.
Judith, daughter of Mr. Collins, Vicar Choral, 17th April, 1667.
Elizabeth, daughter of Mr. William Collins, 6th March, 1704.

MARRIAGES.

Mr. Charles Collins and Mrs. Elizabeth Cardiff, 14th April, 1696.

BURIALS.

———— wife of Mr. William Collins, 10th December, 1650.
Susan, wife of Mr. Richard Collins, 3rd December, 1657.
Mr. George Collins, 10th January, 1669.
Mrs. Collins of St. Olave's Parish, 19th July, 1696.

There are monumental inscriptions in St. Andrew's Church, Chichester, to the Poet's father, mother, maternal uncle, Colonel Martyn, and sister, Mrs. Durnford.

* So much of the will of Colonel Edmund Martyn as relates to the Poet and his sister has been already cited, but the testator's situation in life and the respectability of his family are best shown by other parts of that document. He describes himself as a lieutenant-colonel in his Majesty's service, lying sick in the city of Chichester. To his niece Elizabeth, the wife of Thomas Napper, of Itchenor in Sussex, he bequeathed 100l. His copyhold estates of the manors of Selsey, and Somerly, in that county, to his nephew, Abraham Martyn, the youngest son of his late only brother, Henry Martyn, and to his servant. John Hipp, he gave his wearing apparel and ten pounds.

died. He was an only son : of his two sisters, Elizabeth, the eldest, died unmarried, and Anne, the youngest, who took care of him when he was bereft of reason, married first Mr. Hugh Sempill, who died in 1762, and secondly the Rev. Dr. Thomas Durnford, and died at Chichester in November, 1789. Her character is thus described on the authority of Mr. Park : " The Reverend Mr. Durnford, who resided at Chichester, and was the son of Dr. Durnford, informed me, in August, 1795, that the sister of Collins loved money to excess, and evinced so outrageous an aversion to her brother, because he squandered or gave away to the boys in the cloisters whatever money he had, that she destroyed, in a paroxysm of resentment, all his papers, and whatever remained of his enthusiasm for poetry, as far as she could. Mr. Hayley told me, when I visited him at Eartham, that he had obtained from her a small drawing by Collins, but it possessed no other value than as a memorial that the bard had attempted to handle the pencil as well as the pen." * That Mrs. Durnford was indifferent to her brother's fame, is stated by others, and Sir Egerton Brydges, in his Essay, has made some just observations on the circumstance.

This Memoir must not be closed without an

* Dyce's edition of Collins, 1827, p. 39.

expression of acknowledgment to the Bishop of
Hereford, to the President of Magdalen College,
to H. Gabell, Esq., and to I. Sanden, Esq., of
Chichester, for the desire which they were so
good as to manifest that this account of Collins
might be more satisfactory than it is; and if his
admirers consider that his present biographer has
not done sufficient justice to his memory, an an-
tidote to the injury will be found in the fervent
and unqualified admiration which Sir Egerton
Brydges has evinced for his genius.

AN ESSAY ON THE GENIUS AND POEMS OF COLLINS.

BY SIR EGERTON BRYDGES,

BART.

COLLINS is the founder of a new school of poetry, of a high class. It is true that, unless Buckhurst and Spenser had gone before him, he could not have written as he has done; yet he is an inventor very distinct from both. He calls his odes descriptive and allegorical; and this characterises them truly, but too generally. The personification of abstract qualities had never been so happily executed before; the pure spirituality of the conception, the elegance and force of the language, the harmony and variety of the numbers, were all executed with a felicity which none before or since have reached. That these poems did not at once captivate the public attention cannot be accounted for by any cause hitherto assigned. We may not wonder that the multitude did not at once perceive their full beauties; but that, among readers of taste and learning, there should not have been found a sufficient number to set the example of admiration, is very extraordinary.

In addition to all their other high merits, the mere novelty of thought and manner were sufficient to excite immediate notice. Nor was there any thing in Collins's station or character to create prejudices against the probability that beautiful effusions of genius might be struck out by his hand. His education at the college of Winchester, his fame at Oxford, his associates in London, all were fair preludes to the production of beautiful poetry. Indeed, he had already produced beautiful poetry in his Oriental Eclogues, four years before his Odes appeared. These were, it is admitted, of a different cast from his Odes, and of a gentleness and chastity of thought and diction, which he himself was conscious, some years afterwards, did not very well represent the gorgeousness of eastern composition.

It was a crisis when there was a fair opening for new candidates for the laurel. The uniformity of Pope's style began already to pall upon the public ear. Thomson was indolent, and Young eccentric; Gray had not yet appeared on the stage; and Akenside's metaphysical subject and diffuse style were not calculated to engross the general taste. Johnson had taken possession of the field of satire, but there are too many readers of enthusiastic mind to be satisfied with satire. The pedantry and uncouthness of Walter Harte had precluded him from ever being a fa-

vourite with the public; Shenstone had not yet
risen into fame; and Lyttelton was engrossed by
politics. When, therefore, Collins's Odes ap-
peared, all speculation would have anticipated
that they must have been successful. But we
must recollect that they did not excite the admi-
ration of Johnson; and that Gray did not read
them with that unqualified approval which his
native taste would have inspired. This singu-
larity must be accounted for by other causes
than their want of merit.

The disappointment of Collins was so keen and
deep, that he not only burned the unsold copies
with his own hand, but soon fell into a melan-
choly which ended in insanity. Many persons
have affected to comment on this result with an
unfeeling ignorance of human nature, and, more
especially, of fervid genius. It is, undoubtedly,
highly dangerous to give the entire reins to ima-
gination; the discipline of a constant exercise
of reason is not only salutary, but necessary.
But one can easily conceive how the indulgence
of that state of mind which produced Collins's
Odes could end in an entire overthrow of the
intellect, when embittered by a defect of the
principal objects of his worldly ambition. He is
said to have been puffed up by a vanity which
prompted him to expect that all eyes would be
upon him, and all voices lifted in his praise.
Such was the conception of a vulgar observer of

the human character. Why should it have been
vanity that prompted this hope? It was a con-
sciousness of merit, of those brilliant powers which
produced the Ode to the Passions! was ever a
voice content which sung to those who would not
hear, which was condemned

" To waste its sweetness on the desert air? "

Spenser's power of personification is copious
beyond example; but it is seldom sufficiently
select; rich as it is in imagination, it too com-
monly wants taste and delicacy; it has the fault
of coarseness, which Burke's images in prose two
centuries afterwards, sometimes fell into. But
Collins's images are as pure, and of as exquisite
delicacy, as they are spiritual. They are not
human beings invested with some of the attributes
of angels, but the whole figure is purely angelic,
and of a higher order of creation; in this they
are distinct even from the admirable personifica-
tions of Gray, because they are less earthly. The
Ode to the Passions is, by universal consent,
the noblest of Collins's productions, because it
exhibits a much more extended invention, not of
one passion only, but of all the passions com-
bined, acting, according to the powers of each,
to one end. The execution, also, is the happiest,
each particular passion is drawn with inimitable
force and compression. Let us take only FEAR
and DESPAIR, each dashed out in four lines,

of which every word is like inspiration. Beau-
tiful as Spenser is, and sometimes sublime, yet
he redoubles his touches too much, and often
introduces some coarse feature or expression,
which destroys the spell. Spenser, indeed, has
other merits of splendid and inexhaustible inven-
tion, which render it impossible to put Collins on
a par with him : but we must not estimate merit
by mere quantity: if a poet produces but one
short piece, which is perfect, he must be placed
according to its quality. And surely there is not
a single figure in Collins's Ode to the Passions
which is not perfect, both in conception and
language. He has had many imitators, but no
one has ever approached him in his own depart-
ment.

The Ode to Evening is, perhaps, the next in
point of merit. It is quite of a different cast; it
is descriptive of natural scenery; and such a
scene of enchanting repose was never exhibited
by Claude, or any other among the happiest of
painters. Though a mere verbal description can
never rival a fine picture in a mere address to the
material part of our nature, yet it far eclipses it
with those who have the endowment of a brilliant
fancy, because it gratifies their taste, selection,
and sentiment. Delightful, therefore, as it is to
look upon a Claude, it is more delightful to look
upon this description. It is vain to attempt to
analyse the charm of this Ode; it is so subtle,

that it escapes analysis. Its harmony is so per-
fect, that it requires no rhyme: the objects are
so happily chosen, and the simple epithets convey
ideas and feelings so congenial to each other, as to
throw the reader into the very mood over which
the personified being so beautifully designed pre-
sides. No other poem on the same subject has
the same magic. It assuredly suggested some
images and a tone of expression to Gray in his
Elegy.

The Ode on the Poetical Character is here and
there a little involved and obscure; but its ge-
neral conception is magnificent, and beaming
that spirit of inventive enthusiasm, which alone
can cherish the poet's powers, and bring forth
the due fruits. Collins never touched the lyre
but he was borne away by the inspiration under
which he laboured. The Dirge in Cymbeline,
the lines on Thomson, and the Ode on Colonel
Ross breathe such a beautiful simplicity of pathos,
and yet are so highly poetical and graceful in
every thought and tone, that, exquisitely polished
as they are, and without one superfluous or one
prosaic word, they never once betray the artifices
of composition. The extreme transparency of
the words and thoughts would induce a vulgar
reader to consider them trite, while they are the
expression of a genius so refined as to be all es-
sence of spirit. In Gray, excellent as he is, we
continually encounter the marks of labour and

effort, and occasional crudeness, which shows that effort had not always succeeded, such as "iron hand and torturing hour;" but nothing of this kind occurs in the principal poems of Collins. There is a fire of mind which supersedes labour, and produces what labour cannot. It has been said that Collins is neither sublime nor pathetic; but only ingenious and fanciful. The truth is, that he was cast in the very mould of sublimity and pathos. He lived in an atmosphere above the earth, and breathed only in a visionary world. He was conversant with nothing else, and this must have been the secret by which he produced compositions so entirely spiritual. He who has daily intercourse with the world, and feels the vulgar human passions, cannot be in a humour to write poems which do not partake of earthly coarseness.

It may be asked, *cui bono?* what is the moral use of such poems as these? Whatever refines the intellect improves the heart; whatever augments and fortifies the spiritual part of our nature raises us in the rank of created beings. And what poems are more calculated to refine our intellect, and increase our spirituality, than the poems of Collins? To embody, in a brilliant manner, the most beautiful abstractions, to put them into action, and to add to them splendour, harmony, strength, and purity of language, is to complete a task as admirable for its use and its delight, as

4

it is difficult to be executed. No one can receive the intellectual gratification which such works are capable of producing without being the better for it. The understanding was never yet roused to the conception of such pure and abstract thinking without an elevation of the whole nature of the being so roused. The expression of subtle and evanescent ideas, carried to its perfection, is among the very noblest and most exalted studies with which the human mind can be conversant.

It has been the fashion of our own age to beat out works into twentyfold and fiftyfold the size of those of Collins. I do not quarrel with that fashion; each fashion has its use: and my own taste induces me to perceive the value and many attractions of long narrative poems, full of human passions and practical wisdom. The matter is more desirable than the workmanship; and much of occasional carelessness in the language may be forgiven, for fertility of natural and just thought and interest of story. But this in no degree diminishes the value of those gems, which, though of the smallest size, comprehend perfections of every kind. It is easier to work upon a large field than a small one, — one where is

> " Ample room and verge enough
> The characters of hell to trace."

But these diffuse productions are not calculated to give the same sort of pleasure as the gems.

How difficult was the path chosen by Collins is sufficiently proved by the want of success of all who have entered the same walk: Gray's was not the same, as I shall endeavour presently to show. In the miscellany of Dodsley and other collectors will be found numerous attempts at Allegorical Odes: they are almost all nauseous failures — without originality or distinctness of conception; bald in their language, lame in their numbers, and repulsive from their insipidity of ideas.

Gray's personifications can scarcely be called allegorical, they have so much of humanity about them. He dealt in all the noble and melancholy feelings of the human heart: he never for one moment forgot to be a moralist: he was constantly under the influence of powerful sympathy for the miseries of man's life; and wrote from the overflow of his bosom rather than of his imagination. It is true that his imagination presented the pictures to him; but it was his heart which impelled him to speak. Take the Ode on the Prospect of Eton College; there is not one word which did not break from the bottom of his heart. The multitude cannot enter into the visionary world of Collins: all who have a spark of virtuous human feelings can sympathize with Gray. It is impossible to deny that of these two beautiful poets Gray is the most instructive as a moralist; but Gray is not so original as Collins, not so inventive, not so perfect in his language, and has not so much the fire and flow of inspiration.

When Collins is spoken of as one of the *minor* poets, it is a sad misapplication of the term. Unless he be minor because the number and size of his poems is small, no one is less a minor poet. In him every word is poetry, and poetry either sublime or pathetic. He does not rise to the sublimity of Milton or Dante, or reach the graceful tenderness of Petrarch; but he has a visionary invention of his own, to which there is no rival. As long as the language lasts, every richly gifted and richly cultivated mind will read him with intense and wondering rapture; and will not cease to entertain the conviction, from his example, if from no other, that true poetry of the higher orders is real inspiration.

It will occur to many readers, on perusing these passages of exalted praise, that Johnson has spoken of Collins in a very different manner. Almost fifty years have elapsed since Johnson's final criticism on him appeared in his Lives of the Poets. It disgusted me so much at the time, and the disgust continued so violent, that for a long period it blinded me to all his stupendous merits, because it evinced not only bad taste but unamiable feelings. I cannot yet either justify it, or account for it. He speaks of Collins having sought for splendour without attaining it — of clogging his lines with consonants, and of mistaking inversion of language for poetry. Not one of these faults belongs to Collins. In almost all his poems the words follow their natural order, and are mellifluous beyond those of almost any other verse writer. If the Passions are not described with splendour, there is no such thing as splendour. If the beauties which he sought and attained are unnatural and extravagant, then the tests of correctness and good taste which have been hitherto set up must be abandoned.

This severe criticism is the more extraordinary because Johnson professed a warm personal friendship for Collins; he professes admiration of his talents, learning, and taste, as well as of his disposition and heart, and speaks of his afflicting ill health with a passionate tenderness which has seldom been equalled in beauty, pathos, and force of language. That he could love him personally with such fondness, but be blind to his splendid and unrivaled genius, is utterly beyond my power to account for. Who can say that Johnson wanted taste when we read his sublime and acute criticisms on Milton, Dryden, and Pope? Was it that he roused all the faculties of his judgment when he spoke of these great men of past times; yet, that when he descended to his contemporaries, he indulged his feelings rather than his intellect, and suffered himself to be overcome by the evil passions of envy and contempt? His natural taste was, probably, not the best; when his criticisms were perfect he had tasked his intellect rather than his feelings. He was a man of general wisdom and undoubted genius, but not a very nice scholar, and he prided himself upon his every-day sense, his practical knowledge, rather than those visionary musings which he thought a dangerous indulgence of imagination. He could not put the compositions of Collins among the mere curiosities of literature, but he permitted himself to depreciate habits of mental excursion which he had not himself cultivated.

It was not till more than twenty years after Collins's death that his Ode on the Superstitions of the Highlands was recovered. The two Wartons had seen it, and spoke highly of it to Johnson and others. About 1781, or 1782, a copy was found among the papers of Dr. Carlysle, with a chasm of two or three stanzas. The public deemed it equal to the expectations which had been raised of it; for my part I will confess that I was always deeply disappointed at it. There are in it occasional traces of Collins's genius and several good lines — but none grand — none of that felicitous flow and inspired vigour which mark the Ode to the Passions and other of his lyrics — none of that happy personification of abstract conceptions which is the characteristic of his genius. The majority of the lines lag and

move heavily, and do not seem to me to rise
much above mediocrity in the expression.   The
subject was attractive, and might have afforded
space for the wild excursions of Collins's creative
powers.   As to the edition of Bell, in which it is
pretended that the lost stanzas have been reco-
vered, I have no more doubt that they are *spu-
rious* than that I did not write them myself : I
will not dwell upon this subject, but only men-
tion that it is quite impossible Collins could write
" *Fate* gave the *fatal* blow," and " bowing to
Freedom's *yoke ;* " and such a line as

"In the first year of the first George's reign," &c.

There is not one line among these interpolated
stanzas which it is possible that Collins could
have written.

Mr. Ragdale relates that Collins was in the
habit of writing numerous fragments, and then
throwing them into the flames.   Jackson, of
Exeter, says the same of John Bampfylde.   A
sensitive mind is scarce ever satisfied with the
reception it meets, when, in first heat of compo-
sition, it hopes to delight some listener, to which
it first communicates its new effusions.   It al-
most always considers itself to be " damn'd by
faint praise."   I have known fervid authors who,
if they read or communicated a piece before it
was finished, never went on with it.   They
thought it became blown upon, and turned from

it with coldness, disgust, and despair. Yet the
hearer is commonly not in fault : who can satisfy
the warm hopes of aspiring and restless genius ?

The Wartons have expressed themselves with
praise and affection of Collins, but not, I think,
with the entire admiration which was due to him.
Joseph Warton was a good-natured and generous-
minded man, but something of rivalry lurked in
his bosom ; and the fraternal partiality of Thomas
Warton had the same effect. The younger brother
seems to have thought that Joseph's genius was
equal to that of Collins. Gray had the critical
acumen to discern the difference ; but still he in
no degree does justice to Collins. He accuses
him of want of taste and selection, which is a
surprising charge ; and the more so, because Gray
did not disdain to borrow from him. Gray's
fault was an affected fastidiousness, as appears
by the slighting manner in which he speaks of
Thomson's Castle of Indolence on its first ap-
pearance, as well as of Akenside's Pleasures of
Imagination, and Shenstone's Elegies. That
Gray had exquisite taste, and was a perfect
scholar, no one can doubt.

Collins lived thirteen years after the publication
of his Odes. It does not appear that he pro-
duced any thing after this publication. How
soon his grand mental malady extinguished his
literary powers, I do not exactly know, nor is
it recorded, whether any part of it arose from

bodily disorders. Medical men have never agreed regarding this most deplorable of human afflictions. In Collins's case it probably arose from the mind. On such an intellectual temperament the extinction of the visions which Hope had painted to him seems to have been sufficient to produce that derangement, which first enfeebled, and then perverted and annihilated his faculties. The account given by Johnson is different from that supplied by Mr. Ragdale and another anonymous communication.

He had, perhaps, lucid intervals in which he discovered nothing but weakness and exhaustion. But he appears to have sometimes had fits of violence and despair. It seems that he was an enthusiastic admirer of Shakespeare, and a great reader of black letter books. It may be inferred that his studies were not entirely given up during his malady; but it is a subject of great wonder and regret that the Wartons, the intimate friends both of his better and darker days, have left no particular memorials of him. He had a sister, lately, if not still, living, from whom, though of a very uncongenial nature, something might surely have been gathered. But there is a familiarity which, by destroying admiration, destroys the perception of what will interest others. There are few of our poets of rare genius, of whose private life and character much is known. Little is known of Spenser, Shakespeare, and Milton:

not much even of Thomson. More is known of
Gray by the medium of his beautiful letters;
but when Southey, Wordsworth, and Scott are
gone, posterity will know every particular of
them; and, even now, know much which fills
them with delight and admiration. But let us
know something in good time, also of the new
candidates for poetical fame!

If the life of a poet is not in accordance with
his song, it may be suspected that the song itself
is not genuine. Who can be a poet, and yet be
a worldling in his passions and habits? An arti-
ficial poet is a disgusting dealer in trifles: no-
thing but the predominance of strong and unsti-
mulated feeling will give that inspiration without
which it is worse than an empty sound. When
the passion is factitious, the excitement has al-
ways an immoral tendency; but the delineation
of real and amiable sentiments calls up a sym-
pathy in other bosoms which thus confirms and
fixes them where they would otherwise die away.
The memory may preserve what is artificial, but,
when it becomes stale, it turns to offensiveness,
and thus breeds an alienation from literature
itself.

That Collins has continued to increase in fame
as years have passed away, is the most decisive
of all proofs that his poems have the pure and
sterling merit which began to be ascribed to them
soon after his death. M. Bonstetten tells me

that Gray died without a suspicion of the high
rank he was thereafter to hold in the annals of
British genius? What did poor Collins think
when he submitted his sublime odes to the flames?
He must have had fits of confidence, even then,
in himself; but intermixed with gloom and despair,
and curses of the wretched doom of his birth!
Is it sufficient that a man should wrap himself
up in himself, and be content if the poetry creates
itself and expires in his own heart? We strike
the lyre to excite sympathy, and, if no one will
hear, will any one not feel that he strikes in
vain; and that the talent given us is useless,
and even painful? But who can be assured that
he has the talent if no one acknowledges it?
To have it, and not to be assured that we have
it, is a restless fire that burns to consume us.

Let no one envy the endowments, if he looks
at the fate, of poets. Let him contemplate Spen-
ser, Denham, Rochester, Otway, Collins, Chat-
terton, Burns, Kirke White, Bloomfield, Shelley,
Keats, and Byron, besides those of foreign coun-
tries! Perhaps Collins was the most unhappy of
all; as he was assuredly one of the most inspired
and most amiable.

> " In woful measures wan Despair —
> Low sullen sounds his grief beguiled,
> A solemn, strange, and mingled air ;
> 'Twas sad by fits, by starts 'twas wild."

Langhorne's edition of Collins first appeared in 1765, accompanied by observations which have been generally appended to subsequent editions. These observations have commonly borne the character of feebleness and affectation; they have a sort of pedantic prettiness, which is somewhat repulsive, but they do not want ingenuity, or justness of criticism. Part of them, at least, had previously appeared in the Monthly Review, probably written by Langhorne. Langhorne was not deficient himself in poetical genius, but is principally remembered by a single beautiful stanza, " Cold on Canadian hills," &c. From the time of Langhorne's first edition, Collins became a popular poet; a miniature edition appeared soon after that of Langhorne; and as long as I can remember books, which 'goes back at least to the year 1770, Collins's poems were almost universally on the lips of readers of English poetry. That Cowper, in 1784, should speak of him as " a poet of no great fame," proves nothing, since Cowper's long seclusion from the world had made him utterly ignorant of contemporary literature. The negative inference, from the omission of Beattie, is not of much weight. I cannot recollect the date of the article in the Monthly Review; but, as it appears that Collins survived till 1759, I suspect it was before Collins's death. It was in September, 1754, that the Wartons visited him

at Chichester: in that year he paid a visit to
Oxford, when it appears that he was suffering
under exhausture, not alienation, of mind.

The critics, and, among the rest, Mrs. Bar-
bauld and Campbell, have ascribed to him "fre-
quent obscurity;" this is unjust, — his general
characteristic is lucidness and transparency: he
is never obscure, unless in the Ode to Liberty,
and, perhaps, in a few passages of the Ode on
the Manners. Campbell's criticism is, other-
wise, worthy of this beautiful poet, whom he
praises with congenial spirit. When Hazlitt
speaks of the "tinsel and splendid patchwork"
of Collins, "mixed with the solid, sterling ore of
his genius," he speaks of a base material not to
be found there. In Collins there is no tinsel or
patchwork, one of his excellencies is, that the
whole of every piece is of one web; there are no
joinings or meaner threads. There is no height
to which Collins might not have risen, had he
lived long, had his mind continued sound, and
had he persevered in exercising his genius.
Campbell remarks that, at the same age, Milton
had written nothing which could eclipse his pro-
ductions.

Of the two communications regarding Collins,
to which I have already alluded, one anonymous,
the other by a Mr. John Ragsdale, I must say
something more. The first, signed V., appeared
in the Gentleman's Magazine, with the date of

the 20th Jan. 1781. I well remember its publication, and with what eagerness I read it. I suspect It was at the very crisis of the appearance of the last portion of Johnson's Lives, but possibly a year earlier. I perused it with a mixture of delight, melancholy, and disgust; the first passage which struck me was this: "As he brought with him [to Oxford], for so the whole tone of his conversation discovered, too high an opinion of his school acquisitions and a sovereign contempt for all academic studies and discipline, he never looked with any complacency on his situation in the University, but was always complaining of the dulness of a college life. In short, he threw up his demyship, and going to London, commenced a man of the town, spending his time in all the dissipation of Ranelagh, Vauxhall, and the playhouses; and was romantic enough to suppose that his superior abilities would draw the attention of the great world, by means of whom he was to make his fortune," &c., &c. — "Thus was lost to the world this unfortunate person, in the prime of life, without availing himself of fine abilities, which, if properly improved, must have raised him to the top of any profession, and have rendered him a blessing to his friends, and an ornament to his country."

The vulgarity and narrow-mindedness of this last paragraph filled me with indignation and contempt. In a selfish point of view Collins might, unquestionably, have done better by binding himself to the trammels of a profession; but would he have been more an honor to his friends and an ornament to his country? Are the fruits of genius he has left behind no ornament or use to his country? Professional men, for the most part, live for themselves, and not for the world. Who now remembers Lord Camden, Lord Thurlow, Lord Rosslyn, Lord Kenyon, Lord Ellenborough, or a hundred episcopal or medical characters, all rich and famous in their day?

The character of his person and habits we read with deep interest. "He was passionately fond of music, good-natured, and affable, warm in his friendships, and visionary in his pursuits; and, as long as I knew him, very temperate in his eating and drinking. He was of a moderate stature, of a light and clear complexion, with gray eyes, so very weak at times as hardly to bear a candle in the room, and often raising within him apprehensions of blindness."

The letter from Mr. John Ragsdale is addressed to Mr. William Hymers, Queen's College, Oxford, dated "Hill Street, Richmond, in Surrey, July, 1783." He appears to have been a tradesman in Bond Street; and he surveyed the character of Collins (with whom he was familiar) with a tradesman's eye. He reproached the poet with idleness, not because he was lingering and

losing his time on the road to fame, but because
he omitted to get money by his pen. "To raise
a present subsistence," says Ragsdale, "he set
about writing his Odes; and having a general
invitation to my house, he frequently passed
whole days there, which he employed ,in writing
them, and as frequently burning what he had
written after he had read them to me: many of
them, which pleased me, I struggled to preserve,
but without effect; for, pretending he would
alter them, he got ·them from me, and thrust
them into the fire." That he wrote the Odes to
gain a present subsistence is but the tradesman's
mistaken comment.

Gray was about four years older than Collins,
and he survived him twelve years; he appears to
have spent these years in gloominess and spleen;
but we know not what intense pleasures he re-
ceived from his solitary studies, from the improve-
ment of his mind, from that exquisite taste and
increasing erudition of which every day added to
the stores. The enthusiasm of Collins was more
active and adventurous, and his erudition pro-
bably more acute. Timidity and fastidiousness
were great defects in Gray; they kept down his
invention, and made him resort to the wealth of
others, when he could better have relied upon
himself. But as to borrowing expressions and
simple materials, no genius ever did otherwise;
it is the new and happy combination in which

lies the invention. It may be doubted which are
now most popular, the Odes of Collins or of
Gray.   On the one hand, what is most abstract
is least calculated for the general reader; on the
other hand, the variety of learned allusions in
Gray renders the style and thoughts of his most
celebrated Odes less simple, less direct, and less
easily comprehended at once; but then his deep
morality, the touching strokes which go imme-
diately to the heart, his sensibility to the common
sorrows of human life, his powerful reflection of
the sentiments which " come home to every one's
business and bosom," form an attraction which
perhaps turns the scale in his favour.   Of both
these sublime poets the correctness of compo-
sition renders the writings a national good.

The French Revolution, which affected and
partly reversed the minds of all Europe, produced
a new era in our literature.   There was good as
well as evil in the new force thus infused into the
human intellect.   Our poetry had generally be-
come tame and trite; a sort of languid mechanism
had brought it into contempt; it was very little
read, and still less esteemed.   This might be not
merely the effect, but also the cause of a defi-
ciency of striking genius in the candidates for
the laurel.   Collins and Gray were dead; Mason
had hung up the lyre; and Thomas Warton was
then thought too laboured and quaint; Hayley
had succeeded beyond expectation by a return to

moral and didactic poetry at a moment when the
public was satiated by vile imitations of lyrical
and descriptive composition; but Cowper gave a
new impulse to the curiosity of poetical readers,
by a natural train of thought and the unlaboured
effusions of genuine feeling.   There is no doubt
that a fearful regard to models stifles all force
and preeminent merit.   The burst of the French
Revolution set the faculties of all young persons
free.   It was dangerous to secondary talents, and
only led them into extravagances and absurdi-
ties.   To Wordsworth, Southey, Scott, it was the
removal of a weight, which would have hid the
fire of their genius.   But the exuberance of their
inexhaustible minds in no degree lessens the value
of the more reserved models of excellence of a
tamer age.   The contrast of their varied attrac-
tions supplies the reader with opposite kinds of
merit, which delight and improve the more by
this very opposition.

Authors seldom estimate each other rightly in
their lifetimes.   The race of poets, of whom the
last died with the century, had little friendship,
or even acquaintance among themselves; or
rather, they broke into little sets of two and
three, which narrowed their opinions and their
hearts; Gray and Mason, Johnson and the two
Wartons, Cowper and Hayley, Darwin and Miss
Seward; but Shenstone, Beattie, Akenside, Burns,
Mrs. Carter, Mrs. Smith, &c. stood alone.   This

is not desirable. Innumerable advantages spring
from frank and generous communication. Col-
lins and Gray had not the most remote personal
knowledge of each other. Gray never mentions
Dr. Sneyd Davies, a poet and an Etonian, nearly
contemporary; nor Nicholas Hardinge, a scholar
and a poet also. Mundy, the author of Need-
wood Forest, passed a long life in the country,
totally removed from poets and literati, except
the small coterie of Miss Seward, at Litchfield.
The lives of poets would be the most amusing of
all biography, if the materials were less scanty:
it is strange that so few of them have left any
ample records of themselves; of many not even
a letter or fragment of memorials is preserved.
None of Cowley's letters, a mode of composition
in which he is said to have eminently excelled,
have come down to us. Of Prior, Tickell, Thom-
son, Young, Dyer, Akenside, the Wartons, there
are few of any importance known to be in exist-
ence. Those of Hayley, which Dr. J. Johnson
has brought forward, are not of the interest which
might have been expected. Mrs. Carter's are
excellent, and many of Beattie's amusing and
amiable: it had been well for Miss Seward if
most of hers had been consigned to the flames.
Those of Charlotte Smith it has not been thought
prudent to give to the public. The greater part
of those of Lord Byron, which Moore has hitherto

put forth, had better have been spared: they are written in false taste, and are under a factitious character: in general, the prose style of poets is admirable; — it was not Lord Byron's excellence. We have no specimens of the prose of Collins: it is grievous that he did not execute his project of The History of the Revival of Literature, or of the Lives for the Biographia Britannica, which he undertook. Poets of research are, of all authors, best qualified to write biography with sagacity and eloquence; they see into the human heart, and detect its most secret movements; and if there be a class of literature more amusing and more instructive than another, it is well written biography.

We have a few poets who have not possessed erudition; for genius will overcome all deficiencies of art and labour, such as Shakespeare, Chatterton, Burns, and Bloomfield: but it cannot be questioned that erudition is a mighty aid. Milton could never have been what he was without profound and laborious erudition. Another necessary knowledge is the knowledge of the human heart, which no industry and learning will give. It is an intuitive gift, which mainly depends on an acute and correct imagination, and a sympathetic sensibility of the human passions. Among the innumerable rich endowments of Shakespeare this was the first; it was the predominant brilliance of his knowledge which gave him correctness of description, sentiment, and observation, and clearness, force, and eloquence of language.

Collins had only reached the age of twenty-six when his Odes were published: what inconceivable power would the maturity of age have given him? It is lamentable that he had no familiar friend and companion from that period capable of apprehending and remembering his conversations. In his lucid intervals he must have said many wise, many learned, and many brilliant things; perhaps his very disease, in its vacillation between light and darkness, may have struck out many unexpected and surprising beauties, which common attendants were utterly incapable of appreciating. The flushes of the mind under the unnatural impulses of malady are sometimes inimitably splendid. His reason, at times, was sound, for his reason was fervid to the last. But it is said that his shrieks sometimes resounded through the cathedral cloisters of Chichester till the horror of those who heard him was insupportable.

All these speculations may appear tedious to those whose curiosity is confined to facts: but new facts regarding Collins are not to be had: and what are facts unless they are accompanied by reflections, conclusions, and sentiments? The use of facts is to teach us to think, to judge, and

to feel : and facts, regarding men of genius, are
valuable in enabling us to contemplate how far
the gifts of high intellect contribute to our happi-
ness, or afford guides for the rest of mankind ;
in what respects they have the possessors upon
an equality with the herd of the people; and
where they expose them to temptations from
which others are free. For these purposes the
ill fated Collins is a melancholy illustration : the
Muse had touched the lips of his infancy, and
infused her spirit into him ; she had given him a
piercing understanding, and an amiable disposi-
tion and temper; she enabled him to come forth
with poetry of the first class, in the earliest bloom
of youth ; and to deserve, if not to win, the en-
vied laurel, which millions have reached at in
vain ! What seeming glories and blessings were
these ! Yet to how few was so much misery dis-
pensed as to this once envied being ! May we
not hope that his spirit now has its mighty
reward?

Let it not be denied that there is high virtue in
the culture of the mind, when directed to pure
and elevated objects, and accustoming itself to
travel in lofty paths ! The mind cannot attain
the necessary refinement, nor have its sight
cleared of the film of earthly grossness, unless
the heart throws off the dregs of coarser feeling,
and keeps its wings afloat on a lighter and airier

atmosphere. It may be said, that there have been bad men who have been great poets: but this position remains to be proved. The dissolute men who have written verses have not been great. poets. Were Dante, Petrarch, Tasso, Spenser, Shakespeare, Dryden, Pope, Thomson, Burns, bad men? We know that Milton's character was great and holy, whatever were his politics: and who could be more virtuous than Gray, Beattie, Cowper, and Kirke White? And have we not virtuous poets among the living, — men whose native splendour and intellectual culture have almost purified them into spirits? Let us never cease to meditate on the dejected inspiration, which could pour forth such strains as these :

> " With eyes upraised, as one inspired,
> Pale Melancholy sat retired;
> And from her wild sequester'd seat,
> In notes by distance made more sweet,
> Pour'd through the mellow horn her pensive soul:
> And, dashing soft from rocks around,
> Bubbling runnels join'd the sound;
> Through glades and glooms the mingled measures stole,
> Or o'er some haunted stream with fond delay
> Round a holy calm diffusing,
> Love of peace and lonely musing,
> In hollow murmurs died away."

There are those who will think the praises thus bestowed upon Collins extravagant. It is now sixty years since I became familiar with him; and I still think of him with unabated admiration. When the calm judgment of age confirms the passion of youth and boyhood, we cannot be much mistaken in the merit we ascribe to him who is the object of it.

S. E. B.

ORIENTAL ECLOGUES.

WRITTEN ORIGINALLY FOR THE ENTERTAIN-
MENT OF THE LADIES OF TAURIS.

AND NOW TRANSLATED.

—— Ubi primus equis Oriens adflavit anhelis.

VIRG.

. The First Edition was entitled, "Persian Eclogues, written originally for the Entertainment of the Ladies of Tauris. And now first translated, &c.

Quod si non hic tantus fructus ostenderetur, et si ex his studiis delectatio sola peteretur ; tamen, ut opinor, hanc animi remissionem humanissimam ac liberalissimam judicaretis. Cic. *pro Arch. Poeta.*"

PREFACE.

It is with the writings of mankind, in some measure, as with their complexions or their dress; each nation hath a peculiarity in all these, to distinguish it from the rest of the world.

The gravity of the Spaniard, and the levity of the Frenchman, are as evident in all their productions as in their persons themselves; and the style of my countrymen is as naturally strong and nervous, as that of an Arabian or Persian is rich and figurative.

There is an elegancy and wildness of thought which recommends all their compositions; and our geniuses are as much too cold for the entertainment of such sentiments, as our climate is for their fruits and spices. If any of these beauties are to be found in the following Eclogues, I hope my reader will consider them as an argument of their being original. I received them at the hands of a merchant, who had made it his business to enrich himself with the learning, as well as the silks and carpets of the Persians.

The little information I could gather concerning their author, was, that his name was Abdallah, and that he was a native of Tauris.

It was in that city that he died of a distemper fatal in those parts, whilst he was engaged in celebrating the victories of his favourite monarch, the great Abbas.* As to the Eclogues themselves, they give a very just view of the miseries and inconveniences, as well as the felicities, that attend one of the finest countries in the East.

The time of writing them was probably in the beginning of Sha Sultan Hosseyn's reign, the successor of Sefi or Solyman the Second.

Whatever defects, as, I doubt not, there will be many, fall under the reader's observation, I hope his candour will incline him to make the following reflection:

That the works of Orientals contain many peculiarities, and that, through defect of language, few European translators can do them justice.

* In the Persian tongue, Abbas signifieth "the father of the people."

ORIENTAL ECLOGUES.

ECLOGUE I.

SELIM; OR, THE SHEPHERD'S MORAL.

SCENE, A valley near Bagdat.
TIME, The morning.

'YE Persian maids, attend your poet's lays,
And hear how shepherds pass their golden days.
Not all are blest, whom fortune's hand sustains
With wealth in courts, nor all that haunt the plains:
Well may your hearts believe the truths I tell; 5
'Tis virtue makes the bliss, where'er we dwell.'

Thus Selim sung, by sacred Truth inspired;
Nor praise, but such as Truth bestow'd, desired:
Wise in himself, his meaning songs convey'd ·
Informing morals to the shepherd maid;   10
Or taught the swains that surest bliss to find,
What groves nor streams bestow, a virtuous mind.

When sweet and blushing, like a virgin bride,
The radiant morn resumed her orient pride;
When wanton gales along the valleys play,   15
Breathe on each flower, and bear their sweets away;
By Tigris' wandering waves he sat, and sung
This useful lesson for the fair and young.

'Ye Persian dames,' he said, 'to you belong —
Well may they please — the morals of my song:
No fairer maids, I trust, than you are found,   21
Graced with soft arts, the peopled world around!
The morn that lights you, to your loves supplies
Each gentler ray delicious to your eyes:
For you those flowers her fragrant hands bestow; 25
And yours the love that kings delight to know.
Yet think not these, all beauteous as they are,
The best kind blessings heaven can grant the fair!
Who trust alone in beauty's feeble ray
Boast but the worth * Balsora's pearls display: 30
Drawn from the deep we own their surface bright,
But, dark within, they drink no lustrous light:
Such are the maids, and such the charms they boast,
By sense unaided, or to virtue lost.

VARIATIONS.

Ver. 13. When sweet and odorous, like an eastern bride,
      30. Balsora's pearls have more of worth than they:
      31. Drawn from the deep, they sparkle to the sight,
            And all-unconscious shoot a lustrous light:

* The gulf of that name, famous for the pearl fishery.

Self-flattering sex! your hearts believe in vain 35
That love shall blind, when once he fires, the swain;
Or hope a lover by your faults to win,
As spots on ermine beautify the skin:
Who seeks secure to rule, be first her care
Each softer virtue that adorns the fair; 40
Each tender passion man delights to find,
The loved perfections of a female mind!

'Blest were the days when Wisdom held her
reign,
And shepherds sought her on the silent plain!
With Truth she wedded in the secret grove, 45
Immortal Truth, and daughters bless'd their love.
O haste, fair maids! ye Virtues, come away!
Sweet Peace and Plenty lead you on your way!
The balmy shrub, for you shall love our shore,
By Ind excell'd, or Araby, no more. 50

'Lost to our fields, for so the fates ordain,
The dear deserters shall return again.
Come thou, whose thoughts as limpid springs are
clear,
To lead the train, sweet Modesty, appear:

VARIATIONS.

Ver. 46. The fair-eyed Truth, and daughters bless'd their
love.
53. O come, thou Modesty, as they decree,
The rose may then improve her blush by thee.

Here make thy court amidst our rural scene,   55
And shepherd girls shall own thee for their queen:
With thee be Chastity, of all afraid,
Distrusting all, a wise suspicious maid,
But man the most:—not more the mountain doe
Holds the swift falcon for her deadly foe.   60
Cold is her breast, like flowers that drink the dew;
A silken veil conceals her from the view.
No wild desires amidst thy train be known;
But Faith, whose heart is fix'd on one alone:
Desponding Meekness, with her downcast eyes,
And friendly Pity, full of tender sighs;   66
And Love the last: by these your hearts approve;
These are the virtues that must lead to love.'

   Thus sung the swain; and ancient legends say
The maids of Bagdat verified the lay: .   70
Dear to the plains, the Virtues came along,
The shepherds loved, and Selim bless'd his song.

VARIATION.
Ver. 69. Thus sung the swain, and eastern legends say

ECLOGUE II.

HASSAN; OR, THE CAMEL DRIVER.

SCENE, The desert. TIME, Midday.

In silent horror o'er the boundless waste
The driver Hassan with his camels past:
One cruise of water on his back he bore,
And his light scrip contain'd a scanty store;
A fan of painted feathers in his hand,   5
To guard his shaded face from scorching sand.
The sultry sun had gain'd the middle sky,
.And not a tree, and not an herb was nigh;
The beasts with pain their dusty way pursue; 9
Shrill roar'd the winds, and dreary was the view!
With desperate sorrow wild, the affrighted man
Thrice sigh'd, thrice struck his breast, and thus
     began:
  ' Sad was the hour, and luckless was the day,
  ' When first from Schiraz' walls I bent my way!'

'Ah! little thought I of the blasting wind,   15
The thirst, or pinching hunger, that I find!
Bethink thee, Hassan, where shall thirst assuage,
When fails this cruise, his unrelenting rage?
Soon shall this scrip its precious load resign ;   19
Then what but tears and hunger shall be thine?

   'Ye mute companions of my toils, that bear
In all my griefs a more than equal share!
Here, where no springs in murmurs break away,
Or moss-crown'd fountains mitigate the day,
In vain ye hope the green delights to know,   25
Which plains more blest, or verdant vales bestow:
Here rocks alone, and tasteless sands, are found,
And faint and sickly winds for ever howl around.
   'Sad was the hour, and luckless was the day, 29
   'When first from Schiraz' walls I bent my way!'

   'Curst be the gold and silver which persuade
Weak men to follow far fatiguing trade!
The lily peace outshines the silver store,
And life is dearer than the golden ore :
Yet money tempts us o'er the desert brown,   35
To every distant mart and wealthy town.
Full oft we tempt the land, and oft the sea;
And are we only yet repaid by thee?
Ah! why was ruin so attractive made?
Or why fond man so easily betray'd?   40
Why heed we not, whilst mad we haste along,
The gentle voice of peace, or pleasure's song?

Or wherefore think the flowery mountain's side,
The fountain's murmurs, and the valley's pride,
Why think we these less pleasing to behold   45
Than dreary deserts, if they lead to gold?
  ' Sad was the hour, and luckless was the day,
  ' When first from Schiraz' walls I bent my way!'

  ' O cease, my fears! — all frantic as I go,   49
When thought creates unnumber'd scenes of woe,
What if the lion in his rage I meet! —
Oft in the dust I view his printed feet:
And, fearful! oft, when day's declining light
Yields her pale empire to the mourner night,   54
By hunger roused, he scours the groaning plain,
Gaunt wolves and sullen tigers in his train:
Before them Death with shrieks directs their way,
Fills the wild yell, and leads them to their prey.
  ' Sad was the hour, and luckless was the day, 59
  ' When first from Schiraz' walls I bent my way!'

  ' At that dead hour the silent asp shall creep,
If aught of rest I find, upon my sleep:
Or some swoln serpent twist his scales around,
And wake to anguish with a burning wound.
Thrice happy they, the wise contented poor,   65
From lust of wealth, and dread of death secure!
They tempt no deserts, and no griefs they find;
Peace rules the day, where reason rules the mind.
  ' Sad was the hour, and luckless was the day,
  ' When first from Schiraz' walls I bent my way!'

'O hapless youth!—for she thy love hath won,
The tender Zara will be most undone!
Big swell'd my heart, and own'd the powerful maid,
When fast she dropt her tears, as thus she said:
"Farewell the youth whom sighs could not detain;
Whom Zara's breaking heart implored in vain!
Yet, as thou go'st, may every blast arise
Weak and unfelt, as these rejected sighs!
Safe o'er the wild, no perils mayst thou see,   79
No griefs endure, nor weep, false youth, like me."
O let me safely to the fair return,
Say, with a kiss, she must not, shall not mourn;
O! let me teach my heart to lose its fears,
Recall'd by Wisdom's voice, and Zara's tears.'

He said, and call'd on heaven to bless the day,
When back to Schiraz' walls he bent his way.   86

VARIATION.

Ver. 83.   Go teach my heart to lose its painful fears.

ECLOGUE III.

ABRA; OR, THE GEORGIAN SULTANA.

SCENE, A forest. TIME, The evening.

In Georgia's land, where Tefflis' towers are seen,
In distant view, along the level green,
While evening dews enrich the glittering glade,
And the tall forests cast a longer shade,
What time 'tis sweet o'er fields of rice to stray, 5
Or scent the breathing maize at setting day;
Amidst the maids of Zagen's peaceful grove,
Emyra sung the pleasing cares of love.

Of Abra first began the tender strain,
Who led her youth with flocks upon the plain. 10
At morn she came those willing flocks to lead,
Where lilies rear them in the watery mead;
From early dawn the livelong hours she told,
Till late at silent eve she penn'd the fold.
Deep in the grove, beneath the secret shade, 15
A various wreath of odorous flowers she made:

Verses 5 and 6 were inserted in the second edition.

Gay-motley'd * pinks and sweet jonquils she
    chose,
The violet blue that on the moss-bank grows;
All sweet to sense, the flaunting rose was there;
The finish'd chaplet well adorn'd her hair.   20

    Great Abbas chanced that fated morn to stray,
By love conducted from the chase away;
Among the vocal vales he heard her song,
And sought, the vales and echoing groves amòng;
At length he found, and woo'd the rural maid; 25
She knew the monarch, and with fear obey'd.
    'Be every youth like royal Abbas moved,
    'And every Georgian maid like Abra loved!'

    The royal lover bore her from the plain;
Yet still her crook and bleating flock remain: 30
Oft, as she went, she backward turn'd her view,
And bade that crook and bleating flock adieu.
Fair, happy maid! to other scenes remove,
To richer scenes of golden power and love!
Go leave the simple pipe and shepherd's strain; · 35
With love delight thee, and with Abbas reign!
    'Be every youth like royal Abbas moved,
    'And every Georgian maid like Abra loved!'

---

* That these flowers are found in very great abundance in
some of the provinces of Persia, see the Modern History of
the ingenious Mr. Salmon. C.

Yet, 'midst the blaze of courts, she fix'd her love
On the cool fountain, or the shady grove ;   40
Still, with the shepherd's innocence, her mind
To the sweet vale, and flowery mead, inclined ;
And oft as spring renew'd the plains with flowers,
Breathed his soft gales, and led the fragrant hours,
With sure return she sought the sylvan scene, 45
The breezy mountains, and the forests green.
Her maids around her moved, a duteous band !
Each bore a crook, all rural, in her hand :
Some simple lay, of flocks and herds, they sung ;
With joy the mountain and the forest rung.   50
   ' Be every youth like royal Abbas moved,
   ' And every Georgian maid like Abra loved ! '

   And oft the royal lover left the care
And thorns of state, attendant on the fair ;
Oft to the shades and low-roof'd cots retired, 55
Or sought the vale where first his heart was fired :
A russet mantle, like a swain, he wore,
And thought of crowns, and busy courts, no more.
   ' Be every youth like royal Abbas moved,
   ' And every Georgian maid like Abra loved ! ' 60

   Blest was the life that royal Abbas led :
Sweet was his love, and innocent his bed.
What if in wealth the noble maid excel ?
The simple shepherd girl can love as well.
Let those who rule on Persia's jewel'd throne 65
Be famed for love, and gentlest love alone ;

Or wreathe, like Abbas, full of fair renown,
The lover's myrtle with the warrior's crown.
O happy days! the maids around her say;
O haste, profuse of blessings, haste away!   70
  'Be every youth like royal Abbas moved,
  'And every Georgian maid like Abra loved!'

ECLOGUE IV.

AGIB AND SECANDER; OR, THE FUGITIVES.

SCENE, A mountain in Circassia.

TIME, Midnight.

IN fair Circassia, where, to love inclined,
Each swain was blest, for every maid was kind;
At that still hour, when awful midnight reigns,
And none, but wretches, haunt the twilight plains;
What time the moon had hung her lamp on high, 5
And past in radiance through the cloudless sky;
Sad, o'er the dews, two brother shepherds fled,
Where wildering fear and desperate sorrow led:
Fast as they press'd their flight, behind them lay
Wide ravaged plains, and valleys stole away: 10
Along the mountain's bending sides they ran,
Till, faint and weak, Secander thus began.

SECANDER.

O stay thee, Agib, for my feet deny,
No longer friendly to my life, to fly.
Friend of my heart, O turn thee and survey!   15
Trace our sad flight through all its length of way

And first review that long extended plain,
And yon wide groves, already past with pain!
Yon ragged cliff, whose dangerous path we tried!
And, last, this lofty mountain's weary side!   20

AGIB.

Weak as thou art, yet, hapless, must thou know
The toils of flight, or some severer woe!
Still, as I haste, the Tartar shouts behind,
And shrieks and sorrows load the saddening wind:
In rage of heart, with ruin in his hand,   25
He blasts our harvests, and deforms our land.
Yon citron grove, whence first in fear we came,
Droops its fair honors to the conquering flame:
Far fly the swains, like us, in deep despair,
And leave to ruffian bands their fleecy care.   30

SECANDER.

Unhappy land, whose blessings tempt the sword,
In vain, unheard, thou call'st thy Persian lord!
In vain thou court'st him, helpless, to thine aid,
To shield the shepherd, and protect the maid!
Far off, in thoughtless indolence resign'd,   35
Soft dreams of love and pleasure soothe his mind:
'Midst fair sultanas lost in idle joy,
No wars alarm him, and no fears annoy.

AGIB.

Yet these green hills, in summer's sultry heat,
Have lent the monarch oft a cool retreat.   40

Sweet to the sight is Zabran's flowery plain,
And once by maids and shepherds loved in vain!
No more the virgins shall delight to rove
By Sargis' banks, or Irwan's shady grove;
On Tarkie's mountain catch the cooling gale,   45
Or breathe the sweets of Aly's flowery vale:
Fair scenes! but, ah! no more with peace possest,
With ease alluring, and with plenty blest!
No more the shepherds' whitening tents appear,
Nor the kind products of a bounteous year;   50
No more the date, with snowy blossoms crown'd!
But ruin spreads her baleful fires around.

SECANDER.

In vain Circassia boasts her spicy groves,
For ever famed for pure and happy loves:
In vain she boasts her fairest of the fair,   55
Their eyes' blue languish, and their golden hair!
Those eyes in tears their fruitless grief must send;
Those hairs the Tartar's cruel hand shall rend.

AGIB.

Ye Georgian swains, that piteous learn from far
Circassia's ruin, and the waste of war;   60
Some weightier arms than crooks and staves prepare,
To shield your harvests, and defend your fair:

VARIATIONS.

Ver. 49. No more the shepherds' whitening seats appear,
    51. No more the dale, with snowy blossoms crown'd!

The Turk and Tartar like designs pursue,
Fix'd to destroy, and steadfast to undo.
Wild as his land, in native deserts bred,   65
By lust incited, or by malice led,
The villain Arab, as he prowls for prey,
Oft marks with blood and wasting flames the way;
Yet none so cruel as the Tartar foe,
To death inured, and nurst in scenes of woe.   70

He said; when loud along the vale was heard
A shriller shriek, and nearer fires appear'd :
The affrighted shepherds, through the dews of night,
Wide o'er the moonlight hills renew'd their flight.

END OF THE ECLOGUES.

ODES

ON SEVERAL DESCRIPTIVE AND

ALLEGORICAL SUBJECTS.

Εἴην εὑρυσιεπης ἀναγεισθαι
Προσφορος ἐν Μοισαν διφρῳ :
Τολμα δε και ἀμφιλαφης δυναμις
Εσποιτο.   Πινδαρ. Ολυμπ. Θ.

ODES.

ODE TO PITY.

O THOU, the friend of man, assign'd
With balmy hands his wounds to bind,
   And charm his frantic woe :
When first Distress, with dagger keen,
Broke forth to waste his destined scene,   5
   His wild unsated foe !

By Pella's * bard, a magic name,
By all the griefs his thought could frame,
   Receive my humble rite :
Long, Pity, let the nations view   10
The sky-worn robes of tenderest blue,
   And eyes of dewy light !

---

* Euripides, of whom Aristotle pronounces, on a comparison of him with Sophocles, that he was the greater master of the tender passions, ἦν τραγικώτερος. C.

But wherefore need I wander wide
To old Ilissus' distant side,
   Deserted stream, and mute ?   15
Wild Arun * too has heard thy strains,
And Echo, 'midst my native plains,
   Been soothed by Pity's lute.

There first the wren thy myrtles shed
On gentlest Otway's infant head,   20
   To him thy cell was shown;
And while he sung the female heart,
With youth's soft notes unspoil'd by art,
   Thy turtles mix'd their own.

Come, Pity, come, by Fancy's aid,   25
E'en now my thoughts, relenting maid,
   Thy temple's pride design:
Its southern site, its truth complete,
Shall raise a wild enthusiast heat
   In all who view the shrine.   30

There Picture's toils shall well relate
How chance, or hard involving fate,
   O'er mortal bliss prevail:
The buskin'd Muse shall near her stand,
And sighing prompt her tender hand,   35
   With each disastrous tale.

* The river Arun runs by the village of Trotton in Sussex, where Otway had his birth.

There let me oft, retired by day,
In dreams of passion melt away,
    Allow'd with thee to dwell :
There waste the mournful lamp of night,   40
Till, Virgin, thou again delight
    To hear a British shell !

ODE TO FEAR.

THOU, to whom the world unknown,
With all its shadowy shapes, is shown;
Who seest, appall'd, the unreal scene,
While Fancy lifts the veil between:
 Ah Fear! ah frantic Fear!   5
 I see, I see thee near.
I know thy hurried step, thy haggard eye!
Like thee I start; like thee disorder'd fly.
For, lo, what monsters in thy train appear!
Danger, whose limbs of giant mould   10
What mortal eye can fix'd behold?
Who stalks his round, an hideous form,
Howling amidst the midnight storm;
Or throws him on the ridgy steep
Of some loose hanging rock to sleep: 15
And with him thousand phantoms join'd,
Who prompt to deeds accursed the mind:
And those, the fiends, who, near allied,
O'er Nature's wounds, and wrecks, preside;
Whilst Vengeance, in the lurid air,   20
Lifts her red arm, exposed and bare:
On whom that ravening* brood of Fate,
Who lap the blood of sorrow, wait:

---

* Alluding to the Κύνας ἄφυκτους of Sophocles. See
the Electra. C.

Who, Fear, this ghastly train can see,
And look not madly wild, like thee!　　25

EPODE.

In earliest Greece, to thee, with partial choice,
　The grief-full Muse addrest her infant tongue ;
The maids and matrons, on her awful voice,
　Silent and pale, in wild amazement hung.

Yet he, the bard * who first invoked thy name, 30
　Disdain'd in Marathon its power to feel :
For not alone he nursed the poet's flame,
　But reach'd from Virtue's hand the patriot's
　　steel.

But who is he whom later garlands grace,
　Who left a while o'er Hybla's dews to rove, 35
With trembling eyes thy dreary steps to trace,
　Where thou and faries shared the baleful grove?

Wrapt in thy cloudy veil, the incestuous † queen
　Sigh'd the sad call ‡ her son and husband heard,
When once alone it broke the silent scene,　　40
　And he the wretch of Thebes no more appear'd.

---

* Æschylus. C.　　　　　　　　　† Jocasta. C.
　‡ —— οὐδ' ἔτ' ὠρώρει βοή,
᾿Ην μὲν σιωπή· φθέγμα δ' ἐξαίφνης τινὸς
Θώϋξεν αὐτόν, ὥστε πάντας ὀρθίας
Στῆσαι φόβω δείσαντας ἐξαίφνης τρίχας.
　　　　See the Œdip. Colon. of Sophocles. C.

O Fear, I know thee by my throbbing heart:
 Thy withering power inspired each mournful
  line:
Though gentle Pity claim her mingled part,
 Yet all the thunders of the scene are thine! 45

ANTISTROPHE.

Thou who such weary lengths hast past,
Where wilt thou rest, mad Nymph, at last?
Say, wilt thou shroud in haunted cell,
Where gloomy Rape and Murder dwell?
  Or, in some hollow'd seat,   50
  'Gainst which the big waves beat,
Hear drowning seamen's cries, in tempests brought?
Dark power, with shuddering meek submitted
   thought,
Be mine to read the visions old
Which thy awakening bards have told: 55
And, lest thou meet my blasted view,
Hold each strange tale devoutly true;
Ne'er be I found, by thee o'erawed,
In that thrice hallow'd eve, abroad,
When ghosts, as cottage maids believe,   60
Their pebbled beds permitted leave;
And goblins haunt, from fire, or fen,
Or mine, or flood, the walks of men!

O thou, whose spirit most possest
The sacred seat of Shakespeare's breast!   65

By all that from thy prophet broke,
In thy divine emotions spoke;
Hither again thy fury deal,
Teach me but once like him to feel:
His cypress wreath my meed decree,   70
And I, O Fear, will dwell with thee!

ODE TO SIMPLICITY.

O THOU, by Nature taught
To breathe her genuine thought,
In numbers warmly pure, and sweetly strong;
    Who first, on mountains wild,
    In Fancy, loveliest child,   5
Thy babe, or Pleasure's, nursed the powers of song!

    Thou, who, with hermit heart,
    Disdain'st the wealth of art,
And gauds, and pageant weeds, and trailing pall;
    But com'st a decent maid,   10
    In attic robe array'd,
O chaste, unboastful Nymph, to thee I call!

    By all the honey'd store
    On Hybla's thymy shore;   14
By all her blooms, and mingled murmurs dear;
    By her* whose lovelorn woe,
    In evening musings slow,
Soothed sweetly sad Electra's poet's ear:

---

* The ἀηδών, or nightingale, for which Sophocles seems
to have entertained a peculiar fondness. C.

By old Cephisus deep,
Who spread his wavy sweep,   20
In warbled wanderings, round thy green retreat;
 On whose enamel'd side,
 When holy Freedom died,
No equal haunt allured thy future feet.

 O sister meek of Truth,   25
 To my admiring youth,
Thy sober aid and native charms infuse !
 The flowers that sweetest breathe,
 Though Beauty cull'd the wreath,
Still ask thy hand to range their order'd hues. 30

 While Rome could none esteem
 But virtue's patriot theme,
You lov'd her hills, and led her laureat band:
 But staid to sing alone
 To one distinguish'd throne ;   35
And turn'd thy face, and fled her alter'd land.

 No more, in hall or bower,
 The Passions own thy power,
Love, only Love her forceless numbers mean:
 For thou hast left her shrine ;   40
 Nor olive more, nor vine,
Shall gain thy feet to bless the servile scene.

 Though taste, though genius, bless
 To some divine excess,

Faints the cold work till thou inspire the whole;
  What each, what all supply,   48
  May court, may charm, our eye;
Thou, only thou, canst raise the meeting soul!

  Of these let others ask,
  To aid some mighty task,   50
I only seek to find thy temperate vale;
  Where oft my reed might sound
  To maids and shepherds round,
And all thy sons, O Nature, learn my tale.

ODE ON THE POETICAL CHARACTER.

As once, — if, not with light regard,
I read aright that gifted bard,
— Him whose school above the rest
His loveliest elfin queen has blest; —
One, only one, unrival'd * fair,   5
Might hope the magic girdle wear,
At solemn turney hung on high,
The wish of each love-darting eye;

— Lo! to each other nymph, in turn, applied,
    As if, in air unseen, some hovering hand,   10
Some chaste and angel friend to virgin fame,
    With whisper'd spell had burst the starting band,
It left unblest her loathed dishonour'd side;
    Happier, hopeless Fair, if never
    Her baffled hand, with vain endeavour,   15
Had touch'd that fatal zone to her denied!
Young Fancy thus, to me divinest name,
    To whom, prepared and bathed in heaven,
    The cest of amplest power is given:
    To few the godlike gift assigns,   20
    To gird their blest prophetic loins,
And gaze her visions wild, and feel unmix'd her
        flame!

* Florimel. · See Spenser, Leg. 4th. C.

The band, as fairy legends say,
Was wove on that creating day,
When He, who call'd with thought to birth   25
Yon tented sky, this laughing earth,
And dress'd with springs and forests tall,
And pour'd the main engirting all,
Long by the loved enthusiast woo'd,
Himself in some diviner mood,   30
Retiring, sat with her alone,
And placed her on his sapphire throne;
The whiles, the vaulted shrine around,
Seraphic wires were heard to sound,
Now sublimest triumph swelling,   35
Now on love and mercy dwelling;
And she, from out the veiling cloud,
Breathed her magic notes aloud:
And thou, thou rich-hair'd youth of morn,
And all thy subject life was born !   40
The dangerous passions kept aloof,
Far from the sainted growing woof:
But near it sat ecstatic Wonder,
Listening the deep applauding thunder;
And Truth, in sunny vest array'd,   45
By whose the tarsel's eyes were made;
All the shadowy tribes of mind,
In braided dance, their murmurs join'd,
And all the bright uncounted powers
Who feed on heaven's ambrosial flowers.   50
— Where is the bard whose soul can now
Its high presuming hopes avow?

Where he who thinks, with rapture blind,
This hallow'd work for him design'd?

High on some cliff, to heaven up-piled,   55
Of rude access, of prospect wild,
Where, tangled round the jealous steep,
Strange shades o'erbrow the valleys deep,
And holy Genii guard the rock,
Its glooms embrown, its springs unlock,   60
While on its rich ambitious head,
An Eden, like his own, lies spread:
I view that oak, the fancied glades among,
By which, as Milton lay, his evening ear,
From many a cloud that dropp'd ethereal dew,   65
Nigh sphered in heaven, its native strains could
        hear;
On which that ancient trump he reach'd was hung:
    Thither oft, his glory greeting,
    From Waller's myrtle shades retreating,
With many a vow from Hope's aspiring tongue,
My trembling feet his guiding steps pursue;   71
    In vain — Such bliss to one alone,
    Of all the sons of soul, was known;
    And Heaven, and Fancy, kindred powers,
Have now o'erturn'd the inspiring bowers;   75
Or curtain'd close such scene from every future
        view.

ODE,

WRITTEN IN THE BEGINNING OF THE YEAR 1746.

How sleep the brave, who sink to rest,
By all their country's wishes bless'd!
When Spring, with dewy fingers cold,
Returns to deck their hallow'd mould,
She there shall dress a sweeter sod   5
Than Fancy's feet have ever trod.

By fairy hands their knell is rung;
By forms unseen their dirge is sung;
There Honour comes, a pilgrim gray,
To bless the turf that wraps their clay;   10
And Freedom shall awhile repair,
To dwell a weeping hermit there!

VARIATIONS.

Ver. 5. She then shall dress a sweeter sod
     7. By hands unseen the knell is rung;
     8. By fairy forms their dirge is sung;

ODE TO MERCY.

STROPHE.

O THOU, who sitt'st a smiling bride
By Valour's arm'd and awful side,
Gentlest of sky-born forms, and best adored;
  Who oft with songs, divine to hear,
  Winn'st from his fatal grasp the spear,   5
And hidest in wreaths of flowers his bloodless sword!
  Thou who, amidst the deathful field,
  By godlike chiefs alone beheld,
Oft with thy bosom bare art found,   9
Pleading for him the youth who sinks to ground:
  See, Mercy, see, with pure and loaded hands,
  Before thy shrine my country's genius stands,
And decks thy altar still, though pierced with
     many a wound.

ANTISTROPHE.

When he whom even our joys provoke,
The fiend of nature join'd his yoke,   15
And rush'd in wrath to make our isle his prey;
  Thy form, from out thy sweet abode,
  O'ertook him on his blasted road,
And stopp'd his wheels, and look'd his rage away.

I see recoil his sable steeds, 20
That bore him swift to salvage deeds,
Thy tender melting eyes they own;
O maid, for all thy love to Britain shown,
Where Justice bars her iron tower,
To thee we build a roseate bower; 25
Thou, thou shalt rule our queen, and share our
monarch's throne!

ODE TO LIBERTY.

STROPHE.

Who shall awake the Spartan fife,
And call in solemn sounds to life,
The youths, whose locks divinely spreading,
 Like vernal hyacinths in sullen hue,
At once the breath of fear and virtue shedding, 5
 Applauding Freedom loved of old to view?
What new Alcæus,* fancy-blest,
Shall sing the sword, in myrtles drest,

---

* Alluding to that beautiful fragment of Alcæus:

Εν μύρτου κλαδὶ τὸ ξίφος φορήσω,
Ωσπερ Αρμόδιος κ' Αριστογείτων,
Οτε τὸν τύραννον κτανέτην,
Ισονόμους τ' Αθήνας εποιησάτην.
Φίλταθ' Αρμόδι' οὔ τι που τέθνηκας,
Νήσοις δ' ἐν μακάρων σε φασὶν εἶναι,
Ινα περ ποδώκης Αχιλεὺς,
Τυδείδην τε φασιν Διομήδεα.
Εν μύρτου κλαδὶ τὸ ξίφος φορήσω,
Ωσπερ Αρμόδιος κ' Αριστογείτων,
Οτ' Αθηναίης ἐν θυσίαις
Ανδρα τύραννον Ιππαρχον ἐκαινέτην.
Αεὶ σφῶν κλέος ἔσσεται κατ' αἶαν,
Φίλταθ' Αρμόδιε, κ' Αριστόγειτων,
Οτι τόν τύραννον κτάνετον,
Ισονόμους τ' Αθήνας ἐποιήσατον.

At Wisdom's shrine awhile its flame concealing,
(What place so fit to seal a deed renown'd?)   10
   Till she her brightest lightnings round revealing,
It leap'd in glory forth, and dealt her prompted
     wound!
     O goddess, in that feeling hour,
      When most its sounds would court thy ears,
       Let not my shell's misguided power *   15
      E'er draw thy sad, thy mindful tears.
No, Freedom, no, I will not tell
How Rome, before thy weeping face,
With heaviest sound, a giant-statue, fell,
Push'd by a wild and artless race   20
From off its wide ambitious base,
When Time his northern sons of spoil awoke,
   And all the blended work of strength and grace,
   With many a rude repeated stroke,
And many a barbarous yell, to thousand fragments
     broke.   25

EPODE.

Yet, even where'er the least appear'd,
The admiring world thy hand revered;
Still, 'midst the scatter'd states around,
Some remnants of her strength were found;
They saw, by what escaped the storm,   30
How wondrous rose her perfect form;

---

* Μὴ μὴ ταῦτα λέγωμες, ἃ δάκρυον ἤγαγε Δηοῖ.
           Callimach. Ὕμνος εἰς Δήμητρα. C.

How in the great, the labour'd whole,
Each mighty master pour'd his soul!
For sunny Florence, seat of art,
Beneath her vines preserved a part,   35
Till they,* whom Science loved to name,
(O who could fear it?) quench'd her flame.
And lo, an humbler relic laid
In jealous Pisa's olive shade!
See small Marino† joins the theme,   40
Though least, not last in thy esteem:
Strike, louder strike the ennobling strings
To those,‡ whose merchant sons were kings;
To him,§ who, deck'd with pearly pride,
In Adria weds his green-hair'd bride;   45
Hail, port of glory, wealth, and pleasure,
Ne'er let me change this Lydian measure:
Nor e'er her former pride relate,
To sad Liguria's‖ bleeding state.
Ah no! more pleased thy haunts I seek,   50
On wild Helvetia's¶ mountains bleak:
(Where, when the favour'd of thy choice,
The daring archer heard thy voice;
Forth from his eyrie roused in dread,
The ravening eagle northward fled:)   55

* The family of the Medici. C.
† The little republic of San Marino. C.
‡ The Venetians. C.
§ The Doge of Venice. C.
‖ Genoa. C.   ¶ Switzerland. C.

8

Or dwell in willow'd meads more near,
With those to whom thy stork* is dear:
Those whom the rod of Alva bruised,
Whose crown a British queen† refused !.
The magic works, thou feel'st the strains,   60
One holier name alone remains ;
The perfect spell shall then avail,
Hail, nymph, adored by Britain, hail !

ANTISTROPHE.

Beyond the measure vast of thought,
The works the wizard time has wrought !   65
    The Gaul, 'tis held of antique story,
Saw Britain link'd to his now adverse strand,‡
    No sea between, nor cliff sublime and hoary,
He pass'd with unwet feet through all our land.
    To the blown Baltic then, they say,   70
    The wild waves found another way,

---

* The Dutch, amongst whom there are very severe penalties for those who are convicted of killing this bird. They are kept tame in almost all their towns, and particularly at the Hague, of the arms of which they make a part. The common people of Holland are said to entertain a superstitious sentiment, that if the whole species of them should become extinct, they should lose their liberties. C.

† Queen Elizabeth. C.

‡ This tradition is mentioned by several of our old historians. Some naturalists too have endeavoured to support the probability of the fact by arguments drawn from the correspondent disposition of the two opposite coasts. I do not remember that any poetical use has been hitherto made of it. C.

Where Orcas howls, his wolfish mountains round-
    ing;
Till all the banded west at once 'gan rise,
A wide wild storm even nature's self confounding,
    Withering her giant sons with strange uncouth
      surprise.   75
      This pillar'd earth so firm and wide,
        By winds and inward labours torn,
      In thunders dread was push'd aside,
        And down the shouldering billows borne.
And see, like gems, her laughing train,   80
    The little isles on every side,
Mona,* once hid from those who search the main,
    Where thousand elfin shapes abide,
And Wight who checks the westering tide,
    For thee consenting heaven has each bestow'd, 85
A fair attendant on her sovereign pride:
    To thee this blest divorce she owed,
For thou hast made her vales thy loved, thy last
    abode !

---

* There is a tradition in the Isle of Man, that a mermaid
becoming enamoured of a young man of extraordinary beauty
took an opportunity of meeting him one day as he walked on
the shore, and opened her passion to him, but was received
with a coldness, occasioned by his horror and surprise at her
appearance. This, however, was so misconstrued by the sea
lady, that, in revenge for his treatment of her, she punished
the whole island by covering it with a mist : so that all who
attempted to carry on any commerce with it, either never
arrived at it, but wandered up and down the sea, or were on
a sudden wrecked upon its cliffs. C.

SECOND EPODE.

Then too, 'tis said, an hoary pile,
'Midst the green navel of our isle,⁣ 90
Thy shrine in some religious wood,
O soul-enforcing goddess, stood!
There oft the painted native's feet
Were wont thy form celestial meet:
Though now with hopeless toil we trace 95
Time's backward rolls, to find its place;
Whether the fiery-tresséd Dane,
Or Roman's self o'erturn'd the fane,
Or in what heaven-left age it fell,
'Twere hard for modern song to tell. 100
Yet still, if Truth those beams infuse,
Which guide at once, and charm the Muse,
Beyond yon braided clouds that lie,
Paving the light embroider'd sky,
Amidst the bright pavilion'd plains, 105
The beauteous model still remains.
There, happier than in islands blest,
Or bowers by spring or Hebe drest,
The chiefs who fill our Albion's story,
In warlike weeds, retired in glory, 110
Hear their consorted Druids sing
Their triumphs to the immortal string.
How may the poet now unfold
What never tongue or numbers told?
How learn delighted, and amazed, 115
What hands unknown that fabric raised?

Even now before his favour'd eyes,
In gothic pride, it seems to rise!
Yet Græcia's graceful orders join,
Majestic through the mix'd design:　　　　120
The secret builder knew to choose
Each sphere-found gem of richest hues;
Whate'er heaven's purer mould contains,
When nearer suns emblaze its veins;
There on the walls the patriot's sight　　　125
May ever hang with fresh delight,
And, graved with some prophetic rage,
Read Albion's fame through every age.
　　Ye forms divine, ye laureat band,
That near her inmost altar stand!　　　130
Now soothe her to her blissful train
Blithe Concord's social form to gain;
Concord, whose myrtle wand can steep
Even Anger's bloodshot eyes in sleep;
Before whose breathing bosom's balm　　　135
Rage drops his steel, and storms grow calm:
Her let our sires and matrons hoar
Welcome to Briton's ravaged shore;
Our youths, enamour'd of the fair,
Play with the tangles of her hair,　　　140
Till, in one loud applauding sound,
The nations shout to her around,
O how supremely art thou blest,
Thou, lady — thou shalt rule the west!

ODE TO A LADY,

ON THE DEATH OF COLONEL ROSS, IN THE ACTION OF
FONTENOY.

Written in May, 1745.

WHILE, lost to all his former mirth,
Britannia's genius bends to earth,
    And mourns the fatal day:
While stain'd with blood he strives to tear
Unseemly from his sea-green hair   5
    The wreaths of cheerful May:

The thoughts which musing Pity pays,
And fond Remembrance loves to raise,
    Your faithful hours attend;
Still Fancy, to herself unkind,   10
Awakes to grief the soften'd mind,
    And points the bleeding friend.

By rapid Scheld's descending wave
His country's vows shall bless the grave,

VARIATION.

Ver. 4. While sunk in grief he strives to tear

Where'er the youth is laid :   15
That sacred spot the village hind
With every sweetest turf shall bind,
    And Peace protect the shade.

Blest youth, regardful of thy doom,
Aërial hands shall build thy tomb,   20
    With shadowy trophies crown'd ;
Whilst Honour bathed in tears shall rove
To sigh thy name through every grove,
    And call his heroes round.

The warlike dead of every age,   25
Who fill the fair recording page,
    Shall leave their sainted rest ;
And, half reclining on his spear,
Each wondering chief by turns appear,
    To hail the blooming guest :   30

VARIATIONS.

Ver. 19. E'en now regardful of his doom
    Applauding Honour haunts his tomb,
        With shadowy trophies crown'd :
    Whilst Freedom's form beside her roves,
    Majestic through the twilight groves,
        And calls her heroes round.

19. O'er him, whose doom thy virtues grieve,
    Aërial forms shall sit at eve,
        And bend the pensive head ;
    And, fallen to save his injured land,
    Imperial Honour's awful hand
        Shall point his lonely bed.

Old Edward's sons, unknown to yield,
Shall crowd from Cressy's laurel'd field,
    And gaze with fix'd delight;
Again for Britain's wrongs they feel,
Again they snatch the gleamy steel,   35
    And wish the avenging fight.

But lo, where, sunk in deep despair,
Her garments torn, her bosom bare,
    Impatient Freedom lies!
Her matted tresses madly spread,   40
To every sod, which wraps the dead,
    She turns her joyless eyes.

Ne'er shall she leave that lowly ground
Till notes of triumph bursting round
    Proclaim her reign restored: 45
Till William seek the sad retreat,
And, bleeding at her sacred feet,
    Present the sated sword.

If, weak to soothe so soft a heart,
These pictured glories nought impart,   50
    To dry thy constant tear:
If, yet, in Sorrow's distant eye,
Exposed and pale thou see'st him lie,
    Wild War insulting near:

Ver. 31. Old Edward's sons, untaught to yield,
    49. If, drawn by all a lover's art,

Where'er from time thou court'st relief,   55
The Muse shall still, with social grief,
    Her gentlest promise keep ;
Even humbled Harting's cottaged vale*
Shall learn the sad repeated tale,
    And bid her shepherds weep.   60

VARIATION.

Ver. 58. Even humble Harting's cottaged vale

* Harting, a village adjoining the parish of Trotton, and about two miles distant from it.

ODE TO EVENING.

If aught of oaten stop, or pastoral song,
May hope, chaste Eve, to soothe thy modest ear,
    Like thy own brawling springs,
    Thy springs, and dying gales;   4

O Nymph reserved, while now the bright-hair'd sun
Sits in yon western tent, whose cloudy skirts,
    With brede ethereal wove,
    O'erhang his wavy bed :

Now air is hush'd, save where the weak-eyed bat
With short shrill shriek flits by on leathern wing;
    Or where the beetle winds
    His small but sullen horn,

VARIATIONS.

Ver 2. May hope, O pensive Eve, to soothe thine ear,
   3. Like thy own solemn springs,
   9. While air is hush'd, save where the weak-eyed bat

As oft he rises 'midst the twilight path,
Against the pilgrim borne in heedless hum:
   Now teach me, maid composed,   15
   To breathe some soften'd strain,

Whose numbers, stealing through thy darkening
    vale,
May not unseemly with its stillness suit;
   As, musing slow, I hail
   Thy genial loved return!   20

For when thy folding-star arising shows
His paly circlet, at his warning lamp
   The fragrant Hours, and Elves
   Who slept in buds the day,

And many a Nymph who wreathes her brows with
    sedge,   25
And sheds the freshening dew, and, lovelier still,
   The pensive Pleasures sweet,
   Prepare thy shadowy car.

Then let me rove some wild and heathy scene;
Or find some ruin, 'midst its dreary dells,   30

VARIATIONS.

Ver. 24. Who slept in flowers the day,
    29. Then lead, calm vot'ress, where some sheety lake
       Cheers the lone heath, or some time-hallow'd pile,

Whose walls more awful nod
By thy religious gleams.

Or, if chill blustering winds, or driving rain,
Prevent my willing feet, be mine the hut,
    That, from the mountain's side,   35
    Views wilds, and swelling floods,

And hamlets brown, and dim-discover'd spires;
And hears their simple bell, and marks o'er all
    Thy dewy fingers draw
    The gradual dusky veil.   40

While Spring shall pour his showers, as oft he
      wont,
And bathe thy breathing tresses, meekest Eve !
    While Summer loves to sport
    Beneath thy lingering light;

While sallow Autumn fills thy lap with leaves; 45
Or Winter, yelling through the troublous air,
    Affrights thy shrinking train,
    And rudely rends thy robes;

VARIATIONS.

Ver. 31.   Or upland fallows grey,
            Reflect its last cool gleam.
    33. But when chill blustering winds, or driving rain,
            Forbid my willing feet, be mine the hut,

So long, regardful of thy quiet rule,   49
Shall Fancy, Friendship, Science, smiling Peace,
 Thy gentlest influence own,
 And love thy favourite name!

VARIATION.

Ver. 49. So long, sure-found beneath the sylvan shed,
  Shall Fancy, Friendship, Science, rose-lipp'd Health,
   Thy gentlest influence own,
   And hymn thy favourite name!

ODE TO PEACE.

O THOU, who bad'st thy turtles bear
Swift from his grasp thy golden hair,
  And sought'st thy native skies; .
When War, by vultures drawn from far,
To Britain bent his iron car,   5
  And bade his storms arise !

Tired of his rude tyrannic sway,
Our youth shall fix some festive day,
  His sullen shrines to burn :
But thou who hear'st the turning spheres,   10
What sounds may charm thy partial ears,
  And gain thy blest return !

O Peace, thy injured robes up-bind !
O rise ! and leave not one behind
  Of all thy beamy train ;   15
The British Lion, goddess sweet,
Lies stretch'd on earth to kiss thy feet,
  And own thy holier reign.

Let others court thy transient smile,
But come to grace thy western isle,   20
 By warlike Honour led;
And, while around her ports rejoice,
While all her sons adore thy choice,
 With him for ever wed!

THE MANNERS.

AN ODE.

FAREWELL, for clearer ken design'd,
The dim-discover'd tracts of mind;
Truths which, from action's paths retired,
My silent search in vain required!
No more my sail that deep explores;   5
No more I search those magic shores;
What regions part the world of soul,
Or whence thy streams, Opinion, roll:
If e'er I round such fairy field,
Some power·impart the spear and shield,   10
At which the wizard Passions fly;
By which the giant Follies die!

Farewell the porch whose roof is seen
Arch'd with the enlivening olive's green:
Where Science, prank'd in tissued vest,   15
By Reason, Pride, and Fancy drest,
Comes, like a bride, so trim array'd,
To wed with Doubt in Plato's shade!

Youth of the quick uncheated sight,
Thy walks, Observance, more invite!   20

O thou who lovest that ampler range,
Where life's wide prospects round thee change,
And, with her mingling sons allied,
Throw'st the prattling page aside,
To me, in converse sweet, impart   25
To read in man the native heart;
To learn, where Science sure is found,
From Nature as she lives around;
And, gazing oft her mirror true,
By turns each shifting image view!   30
Till meddling Art's officious lore
Reverse the lessons taught before;
Alluring from a safer rule,
To dream in her enchanted school:
Thou, Heaven, whate'er of great we boast,   35
Hast blest this social science most.

Retiring hence to thoughtful cell,
As Fancy breathes her potent spell,
Not vain she finds the charmful task,
In pageant quaint, in motley mask;   40
Behold, before her musing eyes,
The countless Manners round her rise;
While, ever varying as they pass,
To some Contempt applies her glass:
With these the white-robed maids combine;   45
And those the laughing satyrs join!
But who is he whom now she views,
In robe of wild contending hues?

Thou by the Passions nursed, I greet
The comic sock that binds thy feet!   50
O Humour, thou whose name is known
To Britain's favour'd isle alone:
Me too amidst thy band admit;
There where the young-eyed healthful Wit,
(Whose jewels in his crispéd hair   55
Are placed each other's beams to share;
Whom no delights from thee divide)
In laughter loosed, attends thy side.

By old Miletus,* who so long
Has ceased his love-inwoven song;   60
By all you taught the Tuscan maids,
In changed Italia's modern shades;
By him † whose knight's distinguish'd name
Refined a nation's lust of fame;
Whose tales e'en now, with echoes sweet,   65
Castilia's Moorish hills repeat;
Or him ‡ whom Seine's blue nymphs deplore,
In watchet weeds on Gallia's shore;
Who drew the sad Sicilian maid,
By virtues in her sire betray'd.   70

* Alluding to the Milesian tales, some of the earliest romances. C.

† Cervantes. C.

‡ Monsieur Le Sage, author of the incomparable Adventures of Gil Blas de Santillane, who died in Paris in the year 1745. C.

O Nature boon, from whom proceed
Each forceful thought, each prompted deed;
If but from thee I hope to feel,
On all my heart imprint thy seal!
Let some retreating cynic find 75
Those oft-turn'd scrolls I leave behind:
The Sports and I this hour agree,
To rove thy scene-full world with thee!

THE PASSIONS.

AN ODE FOR MUSIC.

Performed at Oxford, with Hayes's music, in 1750.

When Music, heavenly maid, was young,
While yet in early Greece she sung,
The Passions oft, to hear her shell,
Throng'd around her magic cell,
Exulting, trembling, raging, fainting, 5
Possest beyond the Muse's painting:
By turns they felt the glowing mind
Disturb'd, delighted, raised, refined;
Till once, 'tis said, when all were fired,
Fill'd with fury, rapt, inspired, 10
From the supporting myrtles round
They snatch'd her instruments of sound;
And, as they oft had heard apart
Sweet lessons of her forceful art,
Each (for Madness ruled the hour) 15
Would prove his own expressive power.

First Fear his hand, its skill to try,
 Amid the chords bewilder'd laid,
And back recoil'd, he knew not why,
 E'en at the sound himself had made. 20

Next Anger rush'd ; his eyes on fire,
) In lightnings own'd his secret stings :
In one rude clash he struck the lyre,
    And swept with hurried hand the strings.

With woful measures wan Despair   25
    Low, sullen sounds his grief beguiled ;
A solemn, strange, and mingled air ;
    'Twas sad by fits, by starts 'twas wild.

But thou, O Hope, with eyes so fair,
    What was thy delighted measure ?   30
Still it whisper'd promised pleasure,
    And bade the lovely scenes at distance hail !
Still would her touch the strain prolong ;
    · And from the rocks, the woods, the vale,
She call'd on Echo still, through all the song ; 35
. And, where her sweetest theme she chose,
    A soft responsive voice was heard at every close,
And Hope enchanted smiled, and waved her golden
        hair.
And longer had she sung ; — but, with a frown,
    Revenge impatient rose :   40
He threw his blood-stain'd sword, in thunder,
        down ;
    And, with a withering look,
    The war-denouncing trumpet took,

VARIATION.

Ver. 30. What was thy delightful measure ?

And blew a blast so loud and dread,
Were ne'er prophetic sounds so full of woe!   45
     And, ever and anon, he beat
     The doubling drum, with furious heat;
And though sometimes, each dreary pause between,
     Dejected Pity, at his side,
     Her soul-subduing voice applied,   50
   Yet still he kept his wild unalter'd mein,
While each strain'd ball of sight seem'd bursting
     from his head.
   Thy numbers, Jealousy, to nought were fix'd;
     Sad proof of thy distressful state;   54
   Of differing themes the veering song was mix'd;
     And now it courted Love, now raving call'd
     on Hate.

With eyes upraised, as one inspired,
Pale Melancholy sate retired;
And, from her wild sequester'd seat,
In notes by distance made more sweet,   60
Pour'd through the mellow horn her pensive soul:
     And, dashing soft from rocks around,
     Bubbling runnels join'd the sound;
Through glades and glooms the mingled measure
     stole,   64
   Or, o'er some haunted stream, with fond delay,
     Round an holy calm diffusing,
     Love of Peace, and lonely musing,
   In hollow murmurs died away.

But O! how alter'd was its sprightlier tone,
When Cheerfulness, a nymph of healthiest hue,
 Her bow across her shoulder flung,   71
 Her buskins gemm'd with morning dew,
Blew an inspiring air, that dale and thicket rung,
 The hunter's call, to Faun and Dryad known!
The oak-crown'd Sisters, and their chaste-eyed
   Queen,   75
 Satyrs and Sylvan Boys, were seen,
 Peeping from forth their alleys green:
Brown Exercise rejoiced to hear;
 And Sport leapt up, and seized his beechen spear.
Last came Joy's ecstatic trial: 80
He, with viny crown advancing,
 First to the lively pipe his hand addrest;
But soon he saw the brisk awakening viol,
 Whose sweet entrancing voice he loved the best;
They would have thought who heard the strain 85
 They saw, in Tempe's vale, her native maids,
 Amidst the festal sounding shades,
To some unwearied minstrel dancing,
While, as his flying fingers kiss'd the strings,   89
 Love framed with Mirth a gay fantastic round:
 Loose were her tresses seen, her zone unbound;
 And he, amidst his frolic play,
 As if he would the charming air repay,
Shook thousand odours from his dewy wings.

O Music! sphere-descended maid,   95
Friend of Pleasure, Wisdom's aid!

Why, goddess! why, to us denied,
Lay'st thou thy ancient lyre aside?
As, in that loved Athenian bower,
You learn'd an all commanding power,　　100
Thy mimic soul, O Nymph endear'd,
Can well recall what then it heard;
Where is thy native simple heart,
Devote to Virtue, Fancy, Art?
Arise, as in that elder time,　　105
Warm, energetic, chaste, sublime!
Thy wonders, in that godlike age,
Fill thy recording Sister's page —
'Tis said, and I believe the tale,
Thy humblest reed could more prevail,　　110
Had more of strength, diviner rage,
Than all which charms this laggard age;
E'en all at once together found,
Cecilia's mingled world of sound —
O bid our vain endeavours cease;　　115
Revive the just designs of Greece:
Return in all thy simple state!
Confirm the tales her sons relate!

ODE ON THE DEATH OF THOMSON.

THE SCENE IS SUPPOSED TO
LIE ON THE THAMES NEAR RICHMOND.

In yonder grave a Druid lies,
　Where slowly winds the stealing wave;
The year's best sweets shall duteous rise
　To deck its poet's sylvan grave.

In yon deep bed of whispering reeds　　　　5
　His airy harp* shall now be laid,
That he, whose heart in sorrow bleeds,
　May love through life the soothing shade.

Then maids and youths shall linger here,
　And while its sounds at distance swell,　　10
Shall sadly seem in pity's ear
　To hear the woodland pilgrim's knell.

---

* The harp of Æolus, of which see a description in the
Castle of Indolence. C.

Remembrance oft shall haunt the shore
　　When Thames in summer wreaths is **drest,**
And oft suspend the dashing oar,　　　　15
　　To bid his gentle spirit rest !

And oft, as ease and health retire
　　To breezy lawn, or forest deep,
The friend shall view yon whitening* spire
　　And 'mid the varied landscape weep.　　20

But thou, who own'st that earthy bed,
　　Ah ! what will every dirge avail ;
Or tears, which love and pity shed,
　　That mourn beneath the gliding sail ?

Yet lives there one, whose heedless eye　　25
　　Shall scorn thy pale shrine glimmering near ?
With him, sweet bard, may fancy die,
　　And joy desert the blooming year.

But thou, lorn stream, whose sullen tide
　　No sedge-crown'd sisters now attend,　　30
Now waft me from the green hill's side,
　　Whose cold turf hides the buried friend !

VARIATION.

Ver. 21. But thou who own'st that earthly bed,

* Richmond Church, in which Thomson was buried. C.

And see, the fairy valleys fade;
    Dun night has veil'd the solemn view!
Yet once again, dear parted shade,   35
    Meek Nature's Child, again adieu!

The genial meads,* assign'd to bless
    Thy life, shall mourn thy early doom;
Their hinds and shepherd-girls shall dress,
    With simple hands, thy rural tomb.   40

Long, long, thy stone and pointed clay
    Shall melt the musing Briton's eyes:
O! vales and wild woods, shall he say,
    In yonder grave your Druid lies!

* Mr. Thomson resided in the neighbourhood of Richmond
some time before his death.

ODE ON THE POPULAR SUPERSTITIONS OF THE HIGHLANDS OF SCOTLAND;

CONSIDERED AS THE SUBJECT OF POETRY; INSCRIBED TO MR. JOHN HOME.

I.

HOME, thou return'st from Thames, whose Naiads
    long
  Have seen thee lingering with a fond delay,
  'Mid those soft friends, whose hearts, some fu-
    ture day,
Shall melt, perhaps, to hear thy tragic song.*
Go, not unmindful of that cordial youth †   5
  Whom, long endear'd, thou leavest by Levant's
    side;
Together let us wish him lasting truth,
  And joy untainted with his destined bride.
Go! nor regardless, while these numbers boast
  My short-lived bliss, forget my social name; 10
But think, far off, how, on the southern coast,
  I met thy friendship with an equal flame!

* How truly did Collins predict Home's tragic powers !
† A gentleman of the name of Barrow, who introduced
Home to Collins. Ed. 1788.

Fresh to that soil thou turn'st, where every vale
 Shall prompt the poet, and his song demand:
To thee thy copious subjects ne'er shall fail; 15
 Thou need'st but take thy pencil to thy hand,
And paint what all believe, who own thy genial
   land.

II.

There must thou wake perforce thy Doric quill;
 'Tis Fancy's land to which thou sett'st thy feet;
 Where still, 'tis said, the fairy people meet, 20
Beneath each birken shade, on mead or hill;
There, each trim lass, that skims the milky store,
 To the swart tribes their creamy bowls allots;
By night they sip it round the cottage door,
 While airy minstrels warble jocund notes. 25
There, every herd, by sad experience, knows
 How, wing'd with fate, their elf-shot arrows fly,
When the sick ewe her summer food foregoes,
 Or, stretch'd on earth, the heart-smit heifers
   lie.
Such airy beings awe the untutor'd swain: 30
 Nor thou, though learn'd, his homelier thoughts
   neglect;
Let thy sweet muse the rural faith sustain;
 These are the themes of simple, sure effect,
That add new conquests to her boundless reign,
 And fill, with double force, her heart-command-
   ing strain. 35

III.

E'en yet preserved, how often mayst thou hear,
 Where to the pole the Boreal mountains run,
 Taught by the father, to his listening son,
Strange lays, whose power had charm'd a Spen-
  ser's ear.
At every pause, before thy mind possest,   40
 Old Runic bards shall seem to rise around,
With uncouth lyres, in many-colour'd vest,
 Their matted hair with boughs fantastic crown'd:
Whether thou bidst the well taught hind repeat
 The choral dirge, that mourns some chieftain
  brave,   45
When every shrieking maid her bosom beat,
 And strew'd with choicest herbs his scented
  grave!
Or whether, sitting in the shepherd's shiel,*
 Thou hear'st some sounding tale of war's alarms;
When at the bugle's call, with fire and steel,   50
 The sturdy clans pour'd forth their brawny
  swarms,
And hostile brothers met, to prove each other's
 arms.

VARIATIONS.

Ver. 44. Whether thou bidst the well taught hind relate
   51. The sturdy clans pour'd forth their bony swarms,

* A summer hut, built in the high part of the mountains,
to tend their flocks in the warm season, when the pasture is
fine. Ed. 1788.

IV.

'Tis thine to sing, how, framing hideous spells,
  In Sky's lone isle, the gifted wizard seer,
  Lodged in the wintry cave with Fate's fell spear,
Or in the depth of Uist's dark forest dwells: 56
  How they, whose sight such dreary dreams
      engross,
With their own visions oft astonish'd droop,
  When, o'er the watery strath, or quaggy moss,
They see the gliding ghosts unbodied troop.   60
  Or, if in sports, or on the festive green,
Their destined glance some fated youth descry,
  Who now, perhaps, in lusty vigour seen,
And rosy health, shall soon lamented die.
  For them the viewless forms of air obey;   65
Their bidding heed, and at their beck repair:
  They know what spirit brews the stormful day,
And heartless, oft like moody madness, stare
To see the phantom train their secret work prepare.

V.

To monarchs dear, some hundred miles astray, 70
  Oft have they seen Fate give the fatal blow!
  The seer, in Sky, shriek'd as the blood did flow,
When headless Charles warm on the scaffold lay!

VARIATIONS.

Ver. 56. Or in the gloom of Uist's dark forest dwells:
    58. With their own visions oft afflicted droop,
    66 Their bidding mark, and at their beck repair:

As Boreas threw his young Aurora * forth,
   In the first year of the first George's reign,   75
And battles raged in welkin of the North,
   They mourn'd in air, fell, fell Rebellion slain!
And as, of late, they joy'd in Preston's fight,
   Saw, at sad Falkirk, all their hopes near crown'd!
They raved! divining, through their second sight,†
   Pale, red Culloden, where these hopes were
      drown'd!   81
Illustrious William!‡ Britain's guardian name!
   One William saved us from a tyrant's stroke;
He, for a sceptre, gain'd heroic fame,
   But thou, more glorious, Slavery's chain hast
      broke,   85
To reign a private man, and bow to Freedom's yoke!

VI.

These, too, thou'lt sing! for well thy magic muse
   Can to the topmost heaven of grandeur soar;
Or stoop to wail the swain that is no more!
Ah, homely swains! your homeward steps ne'er
      lose;   90

* By young Aurora, Collins undoubtedly meant the first appearance of the northern lights, which happened about the year 1715; at least it is most highly probable, from this peculiar circumstance, that no ancient writer whatever has taken any notice of them, nor even any modern one, previous to the above period. Ed. 1788.

† Second sight is the term that is used for the divination of the highlanders. Ed. 1788.

‡ The late Duke of Cumberland, who defeated the Pretender at the battle of Culloden. Ed. 1788.

Let not dank Will * mislead you to the heath;
Dancing in mirky night, o'er fen and lake,
He glows, to draw you downward to your death,
In his bewitch'd, low, marshy, willow brake!
What though far off, from some dark dell espied, 95
His glimmering mazes cheer the excursive sight,
Yet turn, ye wanderers, turn your steps aside,
Nor trust the guidance of that faithless light;
For watchful, lurking, 'mid the unrustling reed,
At those mirk hours the wily monster lies, 100
And listens oft to hear the passing steed,
And frequent round him rolls his sullen eyes,
If chance his savage wrath may some weak wretch
surprise.

VII.

Ah, luckless swain, o'er all unblest, indeed!
Whom late bewilder'd in the dank, dark fen, 105
Far from his flocks, and smoking hamlet, then!
To that sad spot where hums the sedgy weed:
On him, enraged, the fiend, in angry mood,
Shall never look with pity's kind concern,
But instant, furious, raise the whelming flood 110
O'er its drown'd banks, forbidding all return!

VARIATION.

Ver. 100. At those sad hours the wily monster lies;
111. O'er its drowned bank, forbidding all return!

* A fiery meteor, called by various names, such as Will
with the Wisp, Jack with the Lantern, etc. It hovers in the
air over marshy and fenny places. Ed. 1788.

ODES.

Or, if he meditate his wish'd escape,
To some dim hill, that seems uprising near,
  To his faint eye the grim and grisly shape,
In all its terrors clad, shall wild appear.   115
  Meantime the watery surge shall round him rise,
Pour'd sudden forth from every swelling source!
  What now remains but tears and hopeless sighs?
His fear-shook limbs have lost their youthly force,
And down the waves he floats, a pale and breath-
          less corse!   120

VIII.

For him in vain his anxious wife shall wait,
  Or wander forth to meet him on his way;
For him in vain at to-fall of the day,
  His babes shall linger at the unclosing gate!
Ah, ne'er shall he return!   Alone, if night   125
  Her travel'd limbs in broken slumbers steep,
With drooping willows drest, his mournful sprite
  Shall visit sad, perchance, her silent sleep:
Then he, perhaps, with moist and watery hand, 129
  Shall fondly seem to press her shuddering cheek,
And with his blue swoln face before her stand,
  And, shivering cold, these piteous accents speak:

VARIATIONS.

Ver. 124. His babes shall linger at the cottage gate!
    127. With dropping willows drest, his mournful sprite
    130. Shall seem to press her cold and shuddering
        cheek,

" Pursue, dear wife, thy daily toils pursue,
    At dawn or dusk, industrious as before ;
Nor e'er of me one helpless thought renew,   135
    While I lie weltering on the osier'd shore,
Drown'd by the Kelpie's * wrath, nor e'er shall aid
    thee more ! "

IX.

Unbounded is thy range ; with varied skill
    Thy muse may, like those feathery tribes which
        spring   139
  From their rude rocks, extend her skirting wing
Round the moist marge of each cold Hebrid isle,
    To that hoar pile † which still its ruins shows :
In whose small vaults a pigmy folk is found,
    Whose bones the delver with his spade upthrows,
And culls them, wondering, from the hallow'd
        ground !   145
Or thither,‡ where, beneath the showery west,
    The mighty kings of three fair realms are laid ;

* The water fiend.

† One of the Hebrides is called the Isle of Pigmies ; where it is reported, that several miniature bones of the human species have been dug up in the ruins of a chapel there.

‡ Icolmkill, one of the Hebrides, where near sixty of the ancient Scottish, Irish, and Norwegian kings are interred.

Once foes, perhaps, together now they rest,
  No slaves revere them, and no wars invade :
Yet frequent now, at midnight's solemn hour,   150
  The rifted mounds their yawning cells unfold,
And forth the monarchs stalk with sovereign power,
  In pageant robes, and wreath'd with sheeny
      gold,
And on their twilight tombs aërial council hold.

X.

But, oh, o'er all, forget not Kilda's race,   155
  On whose bleak rocks, which brave the wasting
      tides,
  Fair Nature's daughter, Virtue, yet abides.
Go! just, as they, their blameless manners trace!
  Then to my ear transmit some gentle song,
Of those whose lives are yet sincere and plain, 160
  Their bounded walks the rugged cliffs along,
And all their prospect but the wintry main.
  With sparing temperance, at the needful time,
They drain the scented spring; or, hunger-prest,
  Along the Atlantic rock, undreading climb, 165
And of its eggs despoil the solan's * nest.

Ver. 164. They drain the sainted spring; or, hunger-prest,

* An aquatic bird like a goose, on the eggs of which the inhabitants of St. Kilda, another of the Hebrides, chiefly subsist. Ed. 1788.

Thus, blest in primal innocence, they live
Sufficed, and happy with that frugal fare
  Which tasteful toil and hourly danger give.
Hard is their shallow soil, and bleak and bare; 170
  Nor ever vernal bee was heard to murmur there!

XI.

Nor need'st thou blush that such false themes
    engage
  Thy gentle mind, of fairer stores possest;
  For not alone they touch the village breast,
But fill'd, in elder time, the historic page.   175
  There, Shakespeare's self, with every garland
    crown'd,
Flew to those fairy climes his fancy sheen,
  In musing hour; his wayward sisters found,
And with their terrors drest the magic scene. 179
  From them he sung, when, 'mid his bold design,
Before the Scot, afflicted, and aghast!
  The shadowy kings of Banquo's fated line
Through the dark cave in gleamy pageant pass'd.
  Proceed! nor quit the tales which, simply told,
Could once so well my answering bosom pierce;
  Proceed, in forceful sounds, and colours bold,
The native legends of thy land rehearse;
To such adapt thy lyre, and suit thy powerful verse.

XII.

In scenes like these, which, daring to depart
  From sober truth, are still to nature true, 190

And call forth fresh delight to Fancy's view.
The heroic muse employ'd her Tasso's art!
    How have I trembled, when, at Tancred's stroke,
Its gushing blood the gaping cypress pour'd!   194
    When each live plant with mortal accents spoke,
And the wild blast upheaved the vanish'd sword!
    How have I sat, when piped the pensive wind,
To hear his harp by British Fairfax strung!
    Prevailing poet! whose undoubting mind
Believed the magic wonders which he sung!   200
    Hence, at each sound, imagination glows!
Hence, at each picture, vivid life starts here!
    Hence his warm lay with softest sweetness flows!
Melting it flows, pure, murmuring, strong, and
        clear,
And fills the impassion'd heart, and wins the
        harmonious ear!   205

VARIATIONS.

Ver. 198. How have I trembled, when, at Tancred's side,
    Like him I stalk'd, and all his passions felt ;
    When charm'd by Ismen, through the forest wide,
    Bark'd in each plant a talking spirit dwelt !

201. Hence, sure to charm, his early numbers flow,
    Though strong, yet sweet——
    Though faithful, sweet ; though strong, of simple
        kind.
    Hence, with each theme, he bids the bosom glow,
    While his warm lays an easy passage find,
    Pour'd through each inmost nerve, and lull the
        harmonious ear.

204. Melting it flows, pure, numerous, strong, and clear,

XIII.

All hail, ye scenes that o'er my soul prevail!
Ye splendid friths and lakes, which, far away,
   Are by smooth Annan * fill'd or pastoral Tay,*
Or Don's * romantic springs at distance hail! 209
The time shall come, when I, perhaps, may tread
   Your lowly glens, o'erhung with spreading
     broom;
Or, o'er your stretching heaths, by Fancy led;
   Or, o'er your mountains creep, in awful gloom!
Then will I dress once more the faded bower, 214
   Where Jonson † sat in Drummond's classic shade;
Or crop, from Tiviotdale, each lyric flower,
   And mourn, on Yarrow's banks, where Willy's
     laid!
Meantime, ye powers that on the plains which bore
   The cordial youth, on Lothian's plains,§ attend!—
Where'er Home dwells, on hill, or lowly moor, 220
   To him I lose, your kind protection lend,
And, touch'd with love like mine, preserve my
   absent friend!

VARIATIONS.

Ver. 216. Or crop from Tiviot's dale each —
     220. Where'er he dwell, on hill, or lowly muir,

 * Three rivers in Scotland. Ed. 1788.

 † Ben Jonson paid a visit on foot, in 1619, to the Scotch
poet Drummond, at his seat of Hawthornden, within four
miles of Edinburgh.

 ‡ Barrow, it seems, was at the Edinburgh University,
which is in the county of Lothian. Ed. 1788.

AN EPISTLE,

ADDRESSED TO SIR THOMAS HANMER, ON HIS EDITION OF
SHAKESPEARE'S WORKS.

SIR,

WHILE, born to bring the Muse's happier days
A patriot's hand protects a poet's lays,
While nursed by you she sees her myrtles bloom,
Green and unwither'd o'er his honour'd tomb;
Excuse her doubts, if yet she fears to tell   5
What secret transports in her bosom swell:
With conscious awe she hears the critic's fame,
And blushing hides her wreath at Shakespeare's
     name.
Hard was the lot those injured strains endured,
Unown'd by Science, and by years obscured: 10

VARIATIONS.

Ver. 1. While, own'd by you, with smiles the Muse surveys
     The expected triumph of her sweetest lays :
     While, stretch'd at ease, she boasts your guardian
       aid,
     Secure, and happy in her sylvan shade:
     Excuse her fears, who scarce a verse bestows,
     In just remembrance of the debt she owes ;
     With conscious, &c.

   9. Long slighted Fancy with a mother's care
     Wept o'er his works, and felt the last despair :
     Torn from her head, she saw the roses fall,
     By all deserted, though admired by all :

Fair Fancy wept; and echoing sighs confess'd
A fix'd despair in every tuneful breast.
Not with more grief the afflicted swains appear,
When wintry winds deform the plenteous year;
When lingering frosts the ruin'd seats invade   15
Where Peace resorted, and the Graces play'd.

Each rising art by just gradation moves,
Toil builds on toil, and age on age improves:
The Muse alone unequal dealt her rage,   19
And graced with noblest pomp her earliest stage.
Preserved through time, the speaking scenes impart
Each changeful wish of Phædra's tortured heart;

VARIATION.

And " Oh ! " she cried, "shall Science still resign
Whate'er is Nature's, and whate'er is mine ?
Shall Taste and Art but show a cold regard,
And scornful Pride reject the unletter'd bard ?
Ye myrtled nymphs, who own my gentle reign,
Tune the sweet lyre, and grace my airy train,
If, where ye rove, your searching eyes have known
One perfect mind, which judgment calls its own;
There every breast its fondest hopes must bend,
And every Muse with tears await her friend."
'Twas then fair Isis from her stream arose,
In kind compassion of her sister's woes.
'Twas then she promised to the mourning maid
The immortal honours which thy hands have paid :
" My best loved son," she said, "shall yet restore
Thy ruin'd sweets, and Fancy weep no more."
Each rising art by slow gradation moves ;
Toil builds, &c.

Or paint the curse that mark'd the Theban's* reign,
A bed incestuous, and a father slain.
With kind concern our pitying eyes o'erflow,   25
Trace the sad tale, and own another's woe.

To Rome removed, with wit secure to please,
The comic Sisters kept their native ease :
With jealous fear, declining Greece beheld
Her own Menander's art almost excell'd ;   30
But every Muse essay'd to raise in vain
Some labour'd rival of her tragic strain :
Ilissus' laurels, though transferr'd with toil,
Droop'd their fair leaves, nor knew the unfriendly
      soil.
As Arts expired, resistless Dulness rose ;   35
Goths, Priests, or Vandals, — all were Learning's
      foes.

VARIATIONS.

Ver. 25. Line after line our pitying eyes o'erflow,
    27. To Rome removed, with equal power to please,
    35. When Rome herself, her envied glories dead,
        No more imperial, stoop'd her conquer'd head ;
        Luxuriant Florence chose a softer theme,
        While all was peace, by Arno's silver stream.
        With sweeter notes the Etrurian vales complain'd,
        And arts reviving told a Cosmo reign'd.
        Their wanton lyres the bards of Provence strung,
        Sweet flow'd the lays, but love was all they sung.
        The gay, &c.

* The Œdipus of Sophocles.

Till Julius * first recall'd each exiled maid,
And Cosmo own'd them in the Etrurian shade :
Then, deeply skill'd in love's engaging theme,
The soft Provençal pass'd to Arno's stream :   40
With graceful ease the wanton lyre he strung ;
Sweet flow'd the lays — but love was all he sung.
The gay description could not fail to move,
For, led by nature, all are friends to love.

But Heaven, still various in its works, decreed 45
The perfect boast of time should last succeed.
The beauteous union must appear at length,
Of Tuscan fancy, and Athenian strength :
One greater Muse Eliza's reign adorn,
And e'en a Shakespeare to her fame be born ! 50

Yet ah ! so bright her morning's opening ray,
In vain our Britain hoped an equal day !
No second growth the western isle could bear,
At once exhausted with too rich a year.
Too nicely Jonson knew the critic's part ;   55
Nature in him was almost lost in art.
Of softer mould the gentle Fletcher came,
The next in order, as the next in name ;
With pleased attention, 'midst his scenes we find
Each glowing thought that warms the female mind ;

VARIATION.

Ver. 45. But Heaven, still rising in its works, decreed

* Julius the Second, the immediate predecessor of Leo the
Tenth.

Each melting sigh, and every tender tear ;   61
The lover's wishes, and the virgin's fear.
His every strain * the Smiles and Graces own ; ·
But stronger Shakespeare felt for man alone :
Drawn by his pen, our ruder passions stand   65
The unrival'd picture of his early hand.

    With † gradual steps and slow, exacter France
Saw Art's fair empire o'er her shores advance :
By length of toil a bright perfection knew,
Correctly bold, and just in all she drew :   70
Till late Corneille, with Lucan's ‡ spirit fired,
Breathed the free strain, as Rome and he inspired :
And classic judgment gain'd to sweet Racine
The temperate strength of Maro's chaster line.

    But wilder far the British laurel spread,   75
And wreaths less artful crown our poet's head.

VARIATIONS.

Ver. 63. His every strain the Loves and Graces own;

71. Till late Corneille from epick Lucan brought
The full expression, and the Roman thought:

   * Their characters are thus distinguished by Mr. Dryden.
   † About the time of Shakespeare, the poet Hardy was in
great repute in France. He wrote, according to Fontenelle,
six hundred plays. The French poets after him applied
themselves in general to the correct improvement of the stage,
which was almost totally disregarded by those of our own
country, Jonson excepted.
   ‡ The favourite author of the elder Corneille.

Yet he alone to every scene could give
The historian's truth, and bid the manners live.
Waked at his call I view, with glad surprise,
Majestic forms of mighty monarchs rise.   80
There Henry's trumpets spread their loud alarms,
And laurel'd Conquest waits her hero's arms.
Here gentler Edward claims a pitying sigh,
Scarce born to honours, and so soon to die!
Yet shall thy throne, unhappy infant, bring   85
No beam of comfort to the guilty king:
The time* shall come when Glo'ster's heart shall
        bleed,
In life's last hours, with horror of the deed;
When dreary visions shall at last present
Thy vengeful image in the midnight tent: 90
Thy hand unseen the secret death shall bear,
Blunt the weak sword, and break the oppressive
        spear!

    Where'er we turn, by Fancy charm'd, we find
Some sweet illusion of the cheated mind.
Oft, wild of wing, she calls the soul to rove   95
With humbler nature, in the rural grove;
Where swains contented own the quiet scene,
And twilight fairies tread the circled green:
Dress'd by her hand, the woods and valleys smile,
And Spring diffusive decks the enchanted isle. 100

---

* Turno tempus erit, magno cum optaverit emptum
    Intactum Pallanta, etc.   VIRG.

O, more than all in powerful genius blest,
Come, take thine empire o'er the willing breast!
Whate'er the wounds this youthful heart shall feel,
Thy songs support me, and thy morals heal!
There every thought the poet's warmth may raise,
There native music dwells in all the lays.   106
O might some verse with happiest skill persuade
Expressive Picture to adopt thine aid!
What wondrous draughts might rise from every
    page!
What other Raphaels charm a distant age!   110

Methinks e'en now I view some free design,
Where breathing Nature lives in every line:

VARIATIONS.

Ver. 101.   O, blest in all that genius gives to charm,
    Whose morals mend us, and whose passions warm!
    Oft let my youth attend thy various page,
    Where rich invention rules the unbounded stage:
    There every scene the poet's warmth may raise,
    And melting music find the softest lays:
    O, might the Muse with equal ease persuade
    Expressive Picture to adopt thine aid!
    Some powerful Raphael should again appear,
    And arts consenting fix their empire here.

111.   Methinks e'en now I view some fair design,
    Where breathing Nature lives in every line;
    Chaste and subdued, the modest colours lie,
    In fair proportion to the approving eye:
    And see where Anthony lamenting stands,
    In fixt distress, and spreads his pleading hands:
    O'er the pale corse the warrior seems to bend,

Chaste and subdued the modest lights decay,
Steal into shades, and mildly melt away.
And see where Anthony,* in tears approved,   115
Guards the pale relics of the chief he loved :
O'er the cold corse the warrior seems to bend,
Deep sunk in grief, and mourns his murder'd friend !
Still as they press, he calls on all around,
Lifts the torn robe, and points the bleeding wound.

But who † is he, whose brows exalted bear   121
A wrath impatient, and a fiercer air ?
Awake to all that injured worth can feel,
On his own Rome he turns the avenging steel ;
Yet shall not war's insatiate fury fall   125
(So heaven ordains it) on the destined wall.
See the fond mother, 'midst the plaintive train,
Hung on his knees, and prostrate on the plain !

VARIATION.

Ver. 122. A rage impatient, and a fiercer air?
           E'en now his thoughts with eager vengeance doom
           The last sad ruin of ungrateful Rome.
           Till, slow advancing o'er the tented plain,
           In sable weeds, appear the kindred train:
           The frantic mother leads their wild despair,
           Beats her swoln breast, and rends her silver hair;
           And see, he yields! the tears unbidden start,
           And conscious nature claims the unwilling heart!
           O'er all the man conflicting passions rise;

* See the tragedy of Julius Cæsar.
† Coriolanus. See Mr. Spence's Dialogue on the Odyssey.

Touch'd to the soul, in vain he strives to hide
The son's affection, in the Roman's pride: 130
O'er all the man conflicting passions rise ;
Rage grasps the sword, while Pity melts the eyes.

   Thus generous Critic, as thy Bard inspires,
The sister Arts shall nurse their drooping fires ;
Each from his scenes her stores alternate bring, 135
Blend the fair tints, or wake the vocal string :
Those sibyl leaves, the sport of every wind,
(For poets ever were a careless kind,)
By thee disposed, no farther toil demand,
But, just to Nature, own thy forming hand.   140

   So spread o'er Greece, the harmonious whole
     unknown,
E'en Homer's numbers charm'd by parts alone.
Their own Ulysses scarce had wander'd more,
By winds and waters cast on every shore :
When, raised by fate, some former Hanmer join'd
Each beauteous image of the boundless mind ; 146
And bade, like thee, his Athens ever claim
A fond alliance with the Poet's name.

  Oxford, Dec. 3,
    1743.

VARIATIONS.

  Ver. 136. Spread the fair tints, or wake the vocal string:
    146. Each beauteous image of the tuneful mind;

DIRGE IN CYMBELINE,

SUNG BY GUIDERUS AND ARVIRAGUS OVER FIDELE,
SUPPOSED TO BE DEAD.

To fair Fidele's grassy tomb
　Soft maids and village hinds shall bring
Each opening sweet of earliest bloom,
　And rifle all the breathing spring.

No wailing ghost shall dare appear　　　　　5
　To vex with shrieks this quiet grove;
But shepherd lads assemble here,
　And melting virgins own their love.

No wither'd witch shall here be seen; ·
　No goblins lead their nightly crew:　　　10
The female fays shall haunt the green,
　And dress thy grave with pearly dew!

VARIATIONS.

Ver. 1. To fair Pastora's grassy tomb
　　7. But shepherd swains assemble here,
　11. But female fays shall haunt the green,
　12. And dress thy bed with pearly dew!

11

The redbreast oft, at evening hours,
  Shall kindly lend his little aid,
With hoary moss, and gather'd flowers,   15
  To deck the ground where thou art laid.

When howling winds, and beating rain,
  In tempests shake the sylvan cell;
Or 'midst the chase, on every plain,
  The tender thought on thee shall dwell; 20

Each lonely scene shall thee restore;
  For thee the tear be duly shed;
Beloved till life can charm no more,
  And mourn'd till Pity's self be dead.

VARIATIONS.

Ver. 17. When chiding winds, and beating rain,
      In tempest shake the sylvan cell;
      Or 'midst the flocks, on every plain,

  21. Each lovely scene shall thee restore;

  23. Beloved till life could charm no more,

VERSES

WRITTEN ON A PAPER WHICH CONTAINED A PIECE OF
BRIDE-CAKE, GIVEN TO THE AUTHOR BY A LADY.

Ye curious hands, that, hid from vulgar eyes,
   By search profane shall find this hallow'd cake,
With virtue's awe forbear the sacred prize,
   Nor dare a theft, for love and pity's sake !

This precious relic, form'd by magic power,   5
   Beneath her shepherd's haunted pillow laid,
Was meant by love to charm the silent hour,
   The secret present of a matchless maid.

The Cyprian queen, at Hymen's fond request,   9
   Each nice ingredient chose with happiest art;
Fears, sighs, and wishes of the enamour'd breast,
   And pains that please, are mix'd in every part.

With rosy hand the spicy fruit she brought,
   From Paphian hills, and fair Cythera's isle; 14
And temper'd sweet with these the melting thought,
   The kiss ambrosial, and the yielding smile.

Ambiguous looks, that scorn and yet relent,
  Denials mild, and firm unalter'd truth;
Reluctant pride, and amorous faint consent,
  And meeting ardours, and exulting youth. 20

Sleep, wayward God! hath sworn, while these re-
    main,
  With flattering dreams to dry his nightly tear,
And cheerful Hope, so oft invoked in vain,
  With fairy songs shall soothe his pensive ear.

If, bound by vows to Friendship's gentle side, 25
  And fond of soul, thou hop'st an equal grace,
If youth or maid thy joys and griefs divide,
  O, much entreated, leave this fatal place!

Sweet Peace, who long hath shunn'd my plain-
    tive day,   '29
  Consents at length to bring me short delight,
Thy careless steps may scare her doves away,
  And Grief with raven note usurp the night.

TO MISS AURELIA C——R,

ON HER WEEPING AT HER SISTER'S WEDDING.

CEASE, fair Aurelia, cease to mourn,
 Lament not Hannah's happy state;
You may be happy in your turn,
 And seize the treasure you regret.

With Love united Hymen stands,   5
 And softly whispers to your charms,
"Meet but your lover in my bands,
 You'll find your sister in his arms."

SONNET.

WHEN Phœbe form'd a wanton smile,
 My soul! it reach'd not here:
Strange, that thy peace, thou trembler, flies
 Before a rising tear!
From 'midst the drops, my love is born,   5
 That o'er those eyelids rove:
Thus issued from a teeming wave
 The fabled queen of love.

SONG.

THE SENTIMENTS BORROWED FROM SHAKESPEARE.*

YOUNG Damon of the vale is dead,
  Ye lowly hamlets, moan ;
A dewy turf lies o'er his head,
  And at his feet a stone.

His shroud, which Death's cold damps destroy,   5
  Of snow-white threads was made :
All mourn'd to see so sweet a boy
  In earth for ever laid.

Pale pansies o'er his corpse were placed,
  Which, pluck'd before their time,   10
Bestrew'd the boy, like him to waste
  And wither in their prime.

VARIATION.

Ver. 2. Ye lowland hamlets, moan ;

* It is uncertain where this poem appeared. It was inserted in the Edinburgh edition of the Poets, 1794. A manuscript copy in the collection recently belonging to Mr. Upcott, and now in the British Museum, is headed, " Written by Collins when at Winchester School. From a Manuscript."

But will he ne'er return, whose tongue
  Could tune the rural lay?
Ah, no! his bell of peace is rung,   15
  · His lips are cold as clay.

They bore him out at twilight hour,
  The youth who loved so well:
Ah, me! how many a true love shower
  Of kind remembrance fell!   20

Each maid was woe — but Lucy chief,
  Her grief o'er all was tried;
Within his grave she dropp'd in grief,
  And o'er her loved one died.

ON OUR LATE TASTE IN MUSIC.*

—— Quid vocis modulamen inane juvabat
Verborum sensusque vacans numerique loquacis?

MILTON.

BRITONS! away with the degenerate pack!
Waft, western winds! the foreign spoilers back!
Enough has been in wild amusements spent,
Let British verse and harmony content!
No music once could charm you like your own,   5
Then tuneful Robinson,† and Tofts were known;
Then Purcell touch'd the strings, while numbers
       hung
Attentive to the sounds — and blest the song!
E'en gentle Weldon taught us manly notes,   9
Beyond the enervate thrills of Roman throats!
Notes, foreign luxury could ne'er inspire,
That animate the soul, and swell the lyre!
That mend, and not emasculate our hearts,
And teach the love of freedom and of arts.   14

* See Memoir, p. xxxviii.
† Now Countess-dowager of Peterborough.

Nor yet, while guardian Phœbus gilds our isle,
Does heaven averse await the muses' toil;
Cherish but once our worth of native race,
The sister-arts shall soon display their face !
Even half discouraged through the gloom they
 strive,
Smile at neglect, and o'er oblivion live. 20
See Handel, careless of a foreign fame,
Fix on our shore, and boast a Briton's name :
While, placed marmoric in the vocal grove,*
He guides the measures listening throngs approve.
Mark silence at the voice of Arne confess'd, 25
Soft as the sweet enchantress rules the breast;
As when transported Venice lent an ear,
Camilla's charms to view, and accents hear ! †
So while she varies the impassion'd song,
Alternate motions on the bosom throng ! 30
As heavenly Milton ‡ guides her magic voice,
And virtue thus convey'd allures the choice.
 Discard soft nonsense in a slavish tongue,
The strain insipid, and the thought unknown ;
From truth and nature form the unerring test ; 35
Be what is manly, chaste, and good the best !
'Tis not to ape the songsters of the groves,
Through all the quiverings of their wanton loves ;
'Tis not the enfeebled thrill, or warbled shake,
The heart can strengthen, or the soul awake ! 40

* Vauxhall.
† Vide the Spectator's Letters from Camilla, vol. vi.
‡ Milton's Comus lately revived.

But where the force of energy is found
When the sense rises on the wings of sound;
When reason, with the charms of music twined,
Through the enraptured ear informs the mind;
Bids generous love or soft compassion glow,   45
And forms a tuneful Paradise below!
  Oh Britons! if the honour still you boast,
No longer purchase follies at such cost!
No longer let unmeaning sounds invite
To visionary scenes of false delight: 50
When, shame to sense! we see the hero's rage
Lisp'd on the tongue, and danced along the stage!
Or hear in eunuch sounds a hero squeak,
While kingdoms rise or fall upon a shake!
Let them at home to slavery's painted train,   55
With siren art, repeat the pleasing strain:
While we, like wise Ulysses, close our ear
To songs which liberty forbids to hear!
Keep, guardian gales, the infectious guests away,
To charm where priests direct, and slaves obey.
Madrid, or wanton Rome, be their delight;
There they may warble as their poets write.
The temper of our isle, though cold, is clear;
And such our genius, noble though severe.   64
Our Shakespeare scorn'd the trifling rules of art,
But knew to conquer and surprise the heart!
In magic chains the captive thought to bind,
And fathom all the depths of human kind!
  Too long, our shame, the prostituted herd
Our sense have bubbled, and our wealth have
        shared.

Too long the favourites of our vulgar great   71
Have bask'd in luxury, and lived in state!
In Tuscan wilds now let them villas rear *
Ennobled by the charity we spare.
There let them warble in the tainted breeze,   75
Or sing like widow'd orphans to the trees:
There let them chant their incoherent dreams,
Where howls Charybdis, and where Scylla screams!
Or where Avernus, from his darksome round,
May echo to the winds the blasted sound!   80
　　As fair Alcyone,† with anguish press'd,
Broods o'er the British main with tuneful breast,
Beneath the white-brow'd cliff protected sings,
Or skims the azure plain with painted wings!
Grateful, like her, to nature, and as just,   85
In our domestic blessings let us trust;
Keep for our sons fair learning's honour'd prize,
Till the world own the worth they now despise!

---

　* Senesino has built a palace near Sienna on an estate
which carries the title of a Marquisate, but purchased with
English gold.
　† The king-fisher.

OBSERVATIONS ON THE ORIENTAL ECLOGUES AND ODES.

BY DR. LANGHORNE.

OBSERVATIONS ON THE ORIENTAL ECLOGUES.

THE genius of the pastoral, as well as of every other respectable species of poetry, had its origin in the east, and from thence was transplanted by the muses of Greece; but whether from the continent of the Lesser Asia, or from Egypt, which, about the era of the Grecian pastoral, was the hospitable nurse of letters, it is not easy to determine. From the subjects, and the manner of Theocritus, one would incline to the latter opinion, while the history of Bion is in favour of the former.

However, though it should still remain a doubt through what channel the pastoral traveled westward, there is not the least shadow of uncertainty concerning its oriental origin.

In those ages which, guided by sacred chronology, from a comparative view of time, we call the early ages, it appears, from the most authentic historians, that the chiefs of the people employed

themselves in rural. exercises, and that astrono-
mers and legislators were at the same time shep-
herds. Thus Strabo informs us, that the history
of the creation was communicated to the Egyp-
tians by a Chaldean shepherd.

From these circumstances it is evident, not only
that such shepherds were capable of all the dig--
nity and elegance peculiar to poetry, but that
whatever poetry they attempted would be of the
pastoral kind; would take its subjects from those
scenes of rural simplicity in which they were con-
versant, and, as it was the offspring of harmony
and nature, would employ the powers it derived
from the former, to celebrate the beauty and be-
nevolence of the latter.

Accordingly we find that the most ancient
poems treat of agriculture, astronomy, and other
objects within the rural and natural systems.

What constitutes the difference between the
georgic and the pastoral, is love and the collo-
quial or dramatic form of composition peculiar to
the latter; this form of composition is sometimes
dispensed with, and love and rural imagery alone
are thought sufficient to distinguish the pastoral.
The tender passion, however, seems to be essen-
tial to this species of poetry, and is hardly ever
excluded from those pieces that were intended to
come under this denomination: even in those
eclogues of the Amœbean kind, whose only pur
port is a trial of skill between contending shep-

herds, love has its usual share, and the praises of
their respective mistresses are the general subjects
of the competitors.

It is to be lamented, that scarce any oriental
compositions of this kind have survived the ra-
vages of ignorance, tyranny, and time; we cannot
doubt that many such have been extant, possibly
as far down as that fatal period, never to be men-
tioned in the world of letters without horror,
when the glorious monuments of human inge-
nuity perished in the ashes of the Alexandrian
library.

Those ingenious Greeks, whom we call the
parents of pastoral poetry, were, probably, no
more than imitators, of imitators that derived
their harmony from higher and remoter sources,
and kindled their poetical fires at those then un-
extinguished lamps which burned within the tombs
of oriental genius.

It is evident that Homer has availed himself of
those magnificent images and descriptions so fre-
quently to be met with in the books of the Old
Testament; and why may not Theocritus, Mos-
chus, and Bion have found their archetypes in
other eastern writers, whose names have perished
with their works? yet, though it may not be
illiberal to admit such a supposition, it would
certainly be invidious to conclude, what the ma-
lignity of cavillers alone could suggest with regard
to Homer, that they destroyed the sources from

12

which they borrowed, and, as it is fabled of the young of the pelican, drained their supporters to death.

As the Septuagint translation of the Old Testament was performed at the request, and under the patronage, of Ptolemy Philadelphus, it were not to be wondered if Theocritus, who was entertained at that prince's court, had borrowed some part of his pastoral imagery from the poetical passages of those books. I think it can hardly be doubted that the Sicilian poet had in his eye certain expressions of the prophet Isaiah, when he wrote the following lines:

Νῦν ἴα μὲν φορέοιτε βάτοι, φορέοιτε δ᾽ ἄκανθαι.
'Α δὲ καλὰ Νάρκισσος ἐπ᾽ ἀρκευθοισι κομάσαι·
Πάντα δ᾽ ἔναλλα γένοιτο, καὶ ἁ πίτυς ὄχνας ἐνείκαι
———— καὶ τὼς κύνας ὤλαφος ἕλκοι.

Let vexing brambles the blue violet bear,
On the rude thorn Narcissus dress his hair,
All, all reversed — The pine with pears be crown'd,
And the bold deer shall drag the trembling hound.

The cause, indeed, of these phenomena is very different in the Greek from what it is in the Hebrew poet; the former employing them on the death, the latter on the birth, of an important person: but the marks of imitation are nevertheless obvious.

It might, however, be expected, that if Theocritus had borrowed at all from the sacred writers, the celebrated pastoral epithalamium of Solomon,

so much within his own walk of poetry, would
not certainly have escaped his notice. His epi-
thalamium on the marriage of Helena, moreover,
gave him an open field for imitation; therefore,
if he has any obligations to the royal bard, we
may expect to find them there. The very open-
ing of the poem is in the spirit of the Hebrew
song:

Οὕτω δὴ πρῶϊζα κατέδραθες, ὦ φίλε γαμβρέ;

The colour of imitation is still stronger in the fol-
lowing passage:

'Αὼς ἀντέλλοισα καλὸν διέφαινε πρόσωπον,
Πότνια νὺξ ἅτε, λευκὸν ἔαρ χειμῶνος ἀνέντος·
῞Ωδε καὶ ἁ χρυσέα ῾Ελένα διεφαίνετ᾽ ἐν ἀμῖν,
Πιείρᾳ μεγάλα ἅτ᾽ ἀνέδραμε κόσμος ἀρούρᾳ.
῾Η κάπῳ κυπάρισσος, ἢ ἅρματι Θεσσαλὸς ἵπποs.

This description of Helen is infinitely above the
style and figure of the Sicilian pastoral: "She is
like the rising of the golden morning, when the
night departeth, and when the winter is over and
gone. She resembleth the cypress in the garden,
the horse in the chariots of Thessaly." These
figures plainly declare their origin; and others,
equally imitative, might be pointed out in the
same idyllium.

This beautiful and luxuriant marriage pastoral
of Solomon is the only perfect form of the orien-
tal eclogue that has survived the ruins of time; a
happiness for which it is, probably, more indebted

to its sacred character than to its intrinsic merit. Not that it is by any means destitute of poetical excellence : like all the eastern poetry, it is bold, wild, and unconnected in its figures, allusions, and parts, and has all that graceful and magnificent daring which characterizes its metaphorical and comparative imagery.

In consequence of these peculiarities, so ill adapted to the frigid genius of the north, Mr. Collins could make but little use of it as a precedent for his Oriental Eclogues ; and even in his third eclogue, where the subject is of a similar nature, he has chosen rather to follow the mode of the Doric and the Latian pastoral.

The scenery and subjects then of the foregoing eclogues alone are oriental ; the style and colouring are purely European ; and, for this reason, the author's preface, in which he intimates that he had the originals from a merchant who traded to the east, is omitted, as being now altogether superfluous.*

With regard to the merit of these eclogues, it may justly be asserted, that in simplicity of description and expression, in delicacy and softness of numbers, and in natural and unaffected tenderness, they are not to be equaled by any thing of the pastoral kind in the English language.

* In the present edition the preface is restored.

ECLOGUE I.

THIS eclogue, which is entitled Selim, or the Shepherd's Moral, as there is nothing dramatic in the subject, may be thought the least entertaining of the four: but it is by no means the least valuable. The moral precepts which the intelligent shepherd delivers to his fellow-swains, and the virgins their companions, are such as would infallibly promote the happiness of the pastoral life.

In impersonating the private virtues, the poet has observed great propriety, and has formed their genealogy with the most perfect judgment, when he represents them as the daughters of truth and wisdom.

The characteristics of modesty and chastity are extremely happy and *peinturesque*:

> " Come thou, whose thoughts as limpid springs are clear,
> To lead the train, sweet Modesty, appear ;
> With thee be Chastity, of all afraid,
> Distrusting all, a wise, suspicious maid ;
> Cold is her breast, like flowers that drink the dew ;
> A silken veil conceals her from the view."

The two similes borrowed from rural objects are not only much in character, but perfectly natural and expressive. There is, notwithstanding, this defect in the former, that it wants a peculiar propriety; for purity of thought may as well be applied to chastity as to modesty; and from this instance, as well as from a thousand more, we may see the necessity of distinguishing, in characteristic poetry, every object by marks and attributes peculiarly its own.

It cannot be objected to this eclogue, that it wants both those essential criteria of the pastoral, love and the drama; for though it partakes not of the latter, the former still retains an interest in it, and that too very material, as it professedly consults the virtue and happiness of the lover, while it informs what are the qualities

——— that must lead to love.

ECLOGUE II.

ALL the advantages that any species of poetry can derive from the novelty of the subject and scenery, this eclogue possesses. The route of a camel-driver is a scene that scarce could exist in the imagination of a European, and of its attendant distresses he could have no idea.—These are very happily and minutely painted by our descriptive poet. What sublime simplicity of expression! what nervous plainness in the opening of the poem!

> "In silent horror o'er the boundless waste
> The driver Hassan with his camels past."

The magic pencil of the poet brings the whole scene before us at once, as it were by enchantment; and in this single couplet we feel all the effect that arises from the terrible wildness of a region unenlivened by the habitations of men. The verses that describe so minutely the camel-driver's little provisions have a touching influence on the imagination, and prepare the reader to

enter more feelingly into his future apprehensions
of distress :

> " Bethink thee, Hassan, where shall thirst assuage,
> When fails this cruise, his unrelenting rage ! "

It is difficult to say whether his apostrophe to the
" mute companions of his toils " is more to be ad-
mired for the elegance and beauty of the poetical
imagery, or for the tenderness and humanity of
the sentiment. He who can read it without being
affected, will do his heart no injustice if he con-
cludes it to be destitute of sensibility :

> " Ye mute companions of my toils, that bear
> In all my griefs a more than equal share !
> Here, where no springs in murmurs break away,
> Or moss-crown'd fountains mitigate the day,
> In vain ye hope the green delights to know,
> Which plains more blest, or verdant vales, bestow :
> Here rocks alone and tasteless sands are found,
> And faint and sickly winds for ever howl around."

Yet in these beautiful lines there is a slight error,
which writers of the greatest genius very fre-
quently fall into. — It will be needless to observe
to the accurate reader, that in the fifth and sixth
verses there is a verbal pleonasm where the poet
speaks of the *green* delights of *verdant* vales.
There is an oversight of the same kind in the
Manners, an Ode, where the poet says,

> " —— Seine's blue nymphs deplore
> In watchet weeds ——."

This fault is indeed a common one, but to a reader of taste it is nevertheless disgustful; and it is mentioned here, as the error of a man of genius and judgment, that men of genius and judgment may guard against it.

Mr. Collins speaks like a true poet, as well in sentiment as expression, when, with regard to the thirst of wealth, he says,

> " Why heed we not, while mad we haste along,
> The gentle voice of Peace, or Pleasure's song?
> Or wherefore think the flowery mountain's side,
> The fountain's murmurs, and the valley's pride,
> Why think we these less pleasing to behold,
> Than dreary deserts, if they lead to gold? "

But however just these sentiments may appear to those who have not revolted from nature and simplicity, had the author proclaimed them in Lombard Street, or Cheapside, he would not have been complimented with the understanding of the bellman. — A striking proof, that our own particular ideas of happiness regulate our opinions concerning the sense and wisdom of others!

It is impossible to take leave of this most beautiful eclogue, without paying the tribute of admiration so justly due to the following nervous lines:

> " What if the lion in his rage I meet! ——
> Oft in the dust I view his printed feet:
> And, fearful! oft, when day's declining light
> Yields her pale empire to the mourner night,

> By hunger roused, he scours the groaning plain,
> Gaunt wolves and sullen tigers in his train:
> Before them death with shrieks directs their way,
> Fills the wild yell, and leads them to their prey."

This, amongst many other passages to be met with in the writings of Collins, shows that his genius was perfectly capable of the grand and magnificent in description, notwithstanding what a learned writer has advanced to the contrary. Nothing, certainly, could be more greatly conceived, or more adequately expressed, than the image in the last couplet.

The deception, sometimes used in rhetoric and poetry, which presents us with an object or sentiment contrary to what we expected, is here introduced to the greatest advantage:

> " Farewell the youth, whom sighs could not detain,
> Whom Zara's breaking heart implored in vain!
> Yet, as thou go'st, may every blast arise ——
> Weak and unfelt as these rejected sighs ! "

But this, perhaps, is rather an artificial prettiness, than a real or natural beauty.

ECLOGUE III.

THAT innocence, and native simplicity of manners, which, in the first eclogue, was allowed to constitute the happiness of love, is here beautifully described in its effects. The sultan of Persia marries a Georgian shepherdess, and finds in her embraces that genuine felicity which unperverted nature alone can bestow. The most natural and beautiful parts of this eclogue are those where the fair sultana refers with so much pleasure to her pastoral amusements, and those scenes of happy innocence in which she had passed her early years; particularly when, upon her first departure,

> " Oft as she went, she backward turned her view,
> And bade that crook and bleating flock adieu."

This picture of amiable simplicity reminds one of that passage where Proserpine, when carried off by Pluto, regrets the loss of the flowers she has been gathering:

> " Collecti flores tunicis excidere remissis:
> Tantaque simplicitas puerilibus adfuit annis,
> Hæc quoque virgineum movit jactura dolorem."

ECLOGUE IV.

THE beautiful but unfortunate country where the scene of this pathetic eclogue is laid, had been recently torn in pieces by the depredations of its savage neighbours, when Mr. Collins so affectingly described its misfortunes. This ingenious man had not only a pencil to portray, but a heart to feel for the miseries of mankind; and it is with the utmost tenderness and humanity he enters into the narrative of Circassia's ruin, while he realizes the scene, and brings the present drama before us. Of every circumstance that could possibly contribute to the tender effect this pastoral was designed to produce, the poet has availed himself with the utmost art and address. Thus he prepares the heart to pity the distresses of Circassia, by representing it as the scene of the happiest love:

> " In fair Circassia, where, to love inclined,
> Each swain was blest, for every maid was kind."

To give the circumstance of the dialogue a more affecting solemnity, he makes the time midnight,

and describes the two shepherds in the very act
of flight from the destruction that swept over
their country:

> " Sad o'er the dews, two brother shepherds fled,
> Where wildering fear and desperate sorrow led."

There is a beauty and propriety in the epithet
wildering, which strikes us more forcibly, the
more we consider it.

The opening of the dialogue is equally happy,
natural, and unaffected; when one of the shep-
herds, weary and overcome with the fatigue of
flight, calls upon his companion to review the
length of way they had passed. This is certainly
painting from nature, and the thoughts, however
obvious, or destitute of refinement, are perfectly
in character. But as the closest pursuit of nature
is the surest way to excellence in general, and to
sublimity in particular, in poetical description, so
we find that this simple suggestion of the shep-
herd is not unattended with magnificence. There
is a grandeur and variety in the landscape he
describes:

> " And first review that long extended plain,
> And yon wide groves, already past with pain!
> Yon ragged cliff, whose dangerous path we tried!
> And, last, this lofty mountain's weary side! "

There is, in imitative harmony, an act of express-
ing a slow and difficult movement by adding to

the usual number of pauses in a verse. This is observable in the line that describes the ascent of the mountain:

And last ‖ this lofty mountain's ‖ weary side ‖.

Here we find the number of pauses, or musical bars, which, in an heroic verse, is commonly two, increased to three.

The liquid melody, and the numerous sweetness of expression, in the following descriptive lines, is almost inimitably beautiful:

" Sweet to the sight is Zabran's flowery plain,
And once by nymphs and shepherds loved in vain!
No more the virgins shall delight to rove
By Sargis' banks, or Irwan's shady grove;
On Tarkie's mountain catch the cooling gale,
Or breathe the sweets of Aly's flowery vale."

Nevertheless, in this delightful landscape there is an obvious fault; there is no distinction between the plain of Zabran and the vale of Aly; they are both flowery, and consequently undiversified. This could not proceed from the poet's want of judgment, but from inattention: it had not occurred to him that he had employed the epithet flowery twice within so short a compass; an oversight which those who are accustomed to poetical, or, indeed, to any other species of composition, know to be very possible.

Nothing can be more beautifully conceived, or more pathetically expressed, than the shepherd's apprehensions for his fair countrywomen, exposed to the ravages of the invaders:

> " In vain Circassia boasts her spicy groves,
> For ever famed for pure and happy loves:
> In vain she boasts her fairest of the fair,
> Their eyes' blue languish, and their golden hair!
> Those eyes in tears their fruitless grief shall send;
> Those hairs the Tartar's cruel hand shall rend."

There is certainly some very powerful charm in the liquid melody of sounds. The editor of these poems could never read or hear the following verse repeated, without a degree of pleasure otherwise entirely unaccountable:

> " Their eyes' blue languish, and their golden hair."

Such are the Oriental Eclogues, which we leave with the same kind of anxious pleasure we feel upon a temporary parting with a beloved friend.

OBSERVATIONS

ON THE ODES, DESCRIPTIVE AND ALLEGORICAL.

THE genius of Collins was capable of every de-
gree of excellence in lyric poetry, and perfectly
qualified for that high province of the muse.
Possessed of a native ear for all the varieties of
harmony and modulation, susceptible of the finest
feelings of tenderness and humanity, but, above
all, carried away by that high enthusiasm which
gives to imagination its strongest colouring, he
was at once capable of soothing the ear with the
melody of his numbers, of influencing the passions
by the force of his pathos, and of gratifying the
fancy by the luxury of description.

In consequence of these powers, but, more
particularly, in consideration of the last, he chose
such subjects for his lyric essays as were most
favourable for the indulgence of description and
allegory; where he could exercise his powers in
moral and personal painting; where he could
exert his invention in conferring new attributes

on images or objects already known, and de-
scribed by a determinate number of characteristics;
where he might give an uncommon éclat to his
figures, by placing them in happier attitudes, or
in more advantageous lights, and introduce new
forms from the moral and intellectual world into
the society of impersonated beings.

Such, no doubt, were the privileges which the
poet expected, and such were the advantages he
derived from the descriptive and allegorical nature
of his themes.

It seems to have been the whole industry of
our author, (and it is, at the same time, almost
all the claim to moral excellence his writings can
boast,) to promote the influence of the social vir-
tues, by painting them in the fairest and happiest
lights.

"Melior fieri tuendo"

would be no improper motto to his poems in
general; but of his lyric poems it seems to be
the whole moral tendency and effect. If, there-
fore, it should appear to some readers, that he
has been more industrious to cultivate description
than sentiment, it may be observed, that his
descriptions themselves are sentimental, and an-
swer the whole end of that species of writing, by
embellishing every feature of virtue, and by con-
veying, through the effects of the pencil, the
finest moral lessons to the mind.

18

Horace speaks of the fidelity of the ear in preference to the uncertainty of the eye; but if the mind receives conviction, it is certainly of very little importance through what medium, or by which of the senses it is conveyed. The impressions left on the imagination may possibly be thought less durable than the deposits of the memory, but it may very well admit of a question, whether a conclusion of reason, or an impression of imagination, will soonest make it sway to the heart. A moral precept, conveyed in words, is only an account of truth in its effects; a moral picture is truth exemplified; and which is most likely to gain upon the affections, it may not be difficult to determine.

This, however, must be allowed, that those works approach the nearest to perfection which unite these powers and advantages; which at once influence the imagination, and engage the memory; the former by the force of animated and striking description, the latter by a brief, but harmonious conveyance of precept: thus, while the heart is influenced through the operation of the passions or the fancy, the effect, which might otherwise have been transient, is secured by the coöperating power of the memory, which treasures up in a short aphorism the moral of the scene.

This is a good reason, and this, perhaps, is the only reason that can be given, why our dramatic

performances should generally end with a chain
of couplets. In these the moral of the whole
piece is usually conveyed; and that assistance
which the memory borrows from rhyme, as it was
probably the original cause of it, gives it useful-
ness and propriety even there.

After these apologies for the descriptive turn
of the following odes, something remains to be
said on the origin and use of allegory in poetical
composition.

By this we are not to understand the trope in
the schools, which is defined aliud verbis, aliud
sensu ostendere; and of which Quintilian says,
usus est, ut tristia dicamus melioribus verbis,
aut bonæ rei gratia quædam contrariis signifi-
cemus, &c. It is not the verbal, but the senti-
mental allegory, not allegorical expression (which,
indeed, might come under the term of metaphor),
but allegorical imagery, that is here in question.

When we endeavour to trace this species of
figurative sentiment to its origin, we find it coeval
with literature itself. It is generally agreed, that
the most ancient productions are poetical; and
it is certain that the most ancient poems abound
with allegorical imagery.

If, then, it be allowed that the first literary
productions were poetical; we shall have little or
no difficulty in discovering the origin of allegory.

At the birth of letters, in the transition from
hieroglyphical to literal expression, it is not to be

wondered if the custom of expressing ideas by personal images, which had so long prevailed, should still retain its influence on the mind, though the use of letters had rendered the practical application of it superfluous. Those who had been accustomed to express strength by the image of an elephant, swiftness by that of a panther, and courage by that of a lion, would make no scruple of substituting, in letters, the symbols for the ideas they had been used to represent.

Here we plainly see the origin of allegorical expression, that it arose from the ashes of hieroglyphics; and if to the same cause we should refer that figurative boldness of style and imagery which distinguish the oriental writings, we shall, perhaps, conclude more justly, than if we should impute it to the superior grandeur of eastern genius.

From the same source with the verbal, we are to derive the sentimental allegory, which is nothing more than a continuation of the metaphorical or symbolical expression of the several agents in an action, or the different objects in a scene.

The latter most peculiarly comes under the denomination of allegorical imagery; and in this species of allegory, we include the impersonation of passions, affections, virtues, and vices, &c. on account of which, principally, the following odes were properly termed, by their author, allegorical.

With respect to the utility of this figurative
writing, the same arguments that have been ad-
vanced in favour of descriptive poetry will be of
weight likewise here. It is, indeed, from imper-
sonation, or, as it is commonly termed, personifi-
cation, that poetical description borrows its chief
powers and graces. Without the aid of this,
moral and intellectual painting would be flat and
unanimated, and even the scenery of material
objects would be dull, without the introduction
of fictitious life.

These observations will be most effectually
illustrated by the sublime and beautiful odes that
occasioned them ; in those it will appear how
happily this allegorical painting may be executed
by the genuine powers of poetical genius, and
they will not fail to prove its force and utility by
passing through the imagination to the heart.

ODE TO PITY.

" By Pella's bard, a magic name,
 By all the griefs his thoughts could frame,
    Receive my humble rite :
Long, Pity, let the nations view
Thy sky-worn robes of tenderest blue,
    And eyes of dewy light ! "

The propriety of invoking Pity, through the
mediation of Euripides, is obvious. — That admi-
rable poet had the keys of all the tender passions,
and therefore could not but stand in the highest
esteem with a writer of Mr. Collins's sensibility.—
He did, indeed, admire him as much as Milton
professedly did, and probably for the same rea-
sons; but we do not find that he has copied him
so closely as the last mentioned poet has some-
times done, and particularly in the opening of
Samson Agonistes, which is an evident imitation
of the following passage in the Phœnissæ :

Ἡγοῦ πάροιθε, θύγατερ, ὡς τυφλῷ ποδὶ
Ὀφθαλμὸς εἶ σύ, ναυτίλοισιν ἄστρον ὥς ·
Δεῦρ' εἰς τὸ λευρὸν πέδον ἴχνος τιθεῖσ' ἐμὸν,
Πρόβαινε ——   Act. III. Sc. I.

The " eyes of dewy light " is one of the happiest

strokes of imagination, and may be ranked among those expressions which

> " — give us back the image of the mind."

> " Wild Arun too has heard thy strains,
> And Echo, 'midst my native plains,
>   Been soothed by Pity's lute."

> " There first the wren thy myrtles shed
> On gentlest Otway's infant head."

Sussex, in which county the Arun is a small river, had the honour of giving birth to Otway as well as to Collins : both these poets, unhappily, became the objects of that pity by which their writings are distinguished. There was a similitude in their genius and in their sufferings. There was a resemblance in the misfortunes and in the dissipation of their lives ; and the circumstances of their death cannot be remembered without pain.

The thought of painting in the temple of Pity the history of human misfortunes, and of drawing the scenes from the tragic muse, is very happy, and in every respect worthy the imagination of Collins.

ODE TO FEAR.

MR. COLLINS, who had often determined to apply himself to dramatic poetry, seems here, with the same view, to have addressed one of the principal powers of the drama, and to implore that mighty influence she had given to the genius of Shakespeare:

> " Hither again thy fury deal,
> Teach me but once like him to feel:
> His cypress wreath my meed decree,
> And I, O Fear, will dwell with thee ! "

In the construction of this nervous ode, the author has shown equal power of judgment and imagination. Nothing can be more striking than the violent and abrupt abbreviation of the measure in the fifth and sixth verses, when he feels the strong influence of the power he invokes:

> " Ah Fear! ah frantic Fear!
> I see, I see thee near."

The editor of these poems has met with nothing in the same species of poetry, either in his own, or in any other language, equal, in all respects, to the following description of Danger:

> " Danger whose limbs of giant mould
> What mortal eye can fix'd behold ?
> Who stalks his round, an hideous form,
> Howling amidst the midnight storm,
> Or throws him on the ridgy steep
> Of some loose hanging rock to sleep."

It is impossible to contemplate the image conveyed in the two last verses, without those emotions of terror it was intended to excite. It has, moreover, the entire advantage of novelty to recommend it; for there is too much originality in all the circumstances, to suppose that the author had in his eye that description of the penal situation of Catiline in the ninth Æneid:

> "——— Te, Catilina, minaci
> Pendentem scopulo."

The archetype of the English poet's idea was in Nature, and, probably, to her alone he was indebted for the thought. From her, likewise, he derived that magnificence of conception, that horrible grandeur of imagery, displayed in the following lines :

> " And those, the fiends, who, near allied,
> O'er Nature's wounds and wrecks preside;
> While Vengeance in the lurid air
> Lifts her red arm, exposed and bare:
> On whom that ravening brood of fate,
> Who lap the blood of sorrow, wait."

That nutritive enthusiasm, which cherishes the

seeds of poetry, and which is, indeed, the only soil wherein they will grow to perfection, lays open the mind to all the influences of fiction. A passion for whatever is greatly wild or magnificent in the works of nature seduces the imagination to attend to all that is extravagant, however unnatural. Milton was notoriously fond of high romance and gothic diableries; and Collins, who in genius and enthusiasm bore no very distant resemblance to Milton, was wholly carried away by the same attachments.

> " Be mine to read the visions old,
> Which thy awakening bards have told:
> And, lest thou meet my blasted view,
> ᵗ Hold each strange tale devoutly true."

> " On that thrice hallow'd eve," &c.

There is an old traditionary superstition, that on St. Mark's eve, the forms of all such persons as shall die within the ensuing year make their solemn entry into the churches of their respective parishes, as St. Patrick swam over the Channel, without their heads.

ODE TO SIMPLICITY

THE measure of the ancient ballad seems to have been made choice of for this ode, on account of the subject; and it has, indeed, an air of simplicity, not altogether unaffecting:

> " By all the honey'd store
> On Hybla's thymy shore,
> By all her blooms, and mingled murmurs dear,
> By her whose love-lorn woe,
> In evening musings slow,
> Sooth'd sweetly sad Electra's poet's ear."

This allegorical imagery of the honeyed store, the blooms, and mingled murmurs of Hybla, alluding to the sweetness and beauty of the Attic poetry, has the finest and the happiest effect: yet, possibly, it will bear a question, whether the ancient Greek tragedians had a general claim to simplicity in any thing more than the plans of their drama. Their language, at least, was infinitely metaphorical; yet it must be owned that they justly copied nature and the passions, and so far, certainly, they were entitled to the palm of true simplicity; the following most beautiful speech

of Polynices will be a monument of this, so long
as poetry shall last:

> ———— πολύδακρυς δ' ἀφικόμην
> Χρόνιος ἰδὼν μέλαθρα, καὶ βωμοὺς θεῶν,
> Γυμνάσιά θ' οἶσιν ἐνετράφην, Δίρκης, θ' ὕδωρ,
> Ὧν οὐ δικαίως ἀπελαθεὶς, ξένην πόλιν
> Ναίω, δι' ὄσσων νᾶμ' ἔχων δακρυρρόουν.
> Ἀλλ' ἐκ γὰρ ἄλγους ἄλγος αὖ, σέ δέρκομαι
> Κάρα ξυρηκὲς, καὶ πέπλους μελαγχίμους
> Ἔχουσαν. Eurip. Phœniss. ver. 869.

> 22 " But staid to sing alone
> 33 To one distinguish'd throne."

The poet cuts off the prevalence of simplicity
among the Romans with the reign of Augustus;
and, indeed, it did not continue much longer,
most of the compositions, after that date, giving
into false and artificial ornament.

> " No more, in hall or bower,
> The passions own thy power,
> Love, only love, her forceless numbers mean."

In these·lines the writings of the Provençal poets
are principally alluded to, in which simplicity is
generally sacrificed to the rhapsodies of romantic
love.

ODE ON THE POETICAL CHARACTER.

Procul ! O ! procul este profani !

THIS ode is so infinitely abstracted and replete
with high enthusiasm, that it will find few readers
capable of entering into the spirit of it, or of
relishing its beauties. There is a style of senti-
ment as utterly unintelligible to common capaci-
ties, as if the subject were treated in an unknown
language ; and it is on the same account that
abstracted poetry will never have many admirers.

The authors of such poems must be content
with the approbation of those heaven-favoured
geniuses, who, by a similarity of taste and senti-
ment, are enabled to penetrate the high mysteries
of inspired fancy, and to pursue the loftiest flights
of enthusiastic imagination. Nevertheless, the
praise of the distinguished few is certainly prefer-
able to the applause of the undiscerning million ;
for all praise is valuable in proportion to the
judgment of those who confer it.

As the subject of this ode is uncommon, so are
the style and expression highly metaphorical and
abstracted : thus the sun is called "the rich-

hair'd youth of morn," the ideas are termed "the shadowy tribes of mind," &c. We are struck with the propriety of this mode of expression here, and it affords us new proofs of the analogy that subsists between language and sentiment.

Nothing can be more loftily imagined than the creation of the cestus of Fancy in this ode: the allegorical imagery is rich and sublime: and the observation, that the dangerous passions kept aloof during the operation, is founded on the strictest philosophical truth: for poetical fancy can exist only in minds that are perfectly serene, and in some measure abstracted from the influences of sense.

The scene of Milton's "inspiring hour" is perfectly in character, and described with all those wild-wood appearances of which the great poet was so enthusiastically fond:

"I view that oak, the fancied glades among,
By which as Milton lay, his evening ear,
Nigh sphered in heaven, its native strains could hear."

ODE,

WRITTEN IN THE YEAR 1746.

ODE TO MERCY.

THE Ode written in 1746, and the Ode to Mercy, seem to have been written on the same occasion, viz. the late rebellion; the former in memory of those heroes who fell in defence of their country, the latter to excite sentiments of compassion in favour of those unhappy and deluded wretches who became a sacrifice to public justice.

The language and imagery of both are very beautiful; but the scene and figures described, in the strophe of the Ode to Mercy, are exquisitely striking, and would afford a painter one of the finest subjects in the world.

ODE TO LIBERTY.

THE ancient states of Greece, perhaps the only ones in which a perfect model of liberty ever existed, are naturally brought to view in the opening of the poem:

> " Who shall awake the Spartan fife,
> And call in solemn sounds to life,
> The youths, whose locks divinely spreading,
> Like vernal hyacinths in sullen hue. "

There is something extremely bold in this imagery of the locks of the Spartan youths, and greatly superior to that description Jocasta gives us of the hair of Polynices:

> Βοστρύχων τε κυανόχρωτα χαίτας
> Πλόκαμον ———

> " What new Alcæus, fancy-blest,
> Shall sing the sword, in myrtles drest," &c.

This alludes to a fragment of Alcæus still remaining, in which the poet celebrates Harmodius and Aristogiton, who slew the tyrant Hipparchus, and thereby restored the liberty of Athens.

The fall of Rome is here most nervously described in one line

> " With heaviest sound, a giant statue, fell."

The thought seems altogether new, and the imitative harmony in the structure of the verse is admirable.

After bewailing the ruin of ancient liberty, the poet considers the influence it has retained, or still retains, among the moderns; and here the free republics of Italy naturally engage his attention. — Florence, indeed, only to be lamented on account of losing its liberty under those patrons of letters, the Medicean family; the jealous Pisa, justly so called, in respect to its long impatience and regret under the same yoke; and the small Marino, which, however unrespectable with regard to power or extent of territory, has, at least, this distinction to boast, that it has preserved its liberty longer than any other state, ancient or modern, having, without any revolution, retained its present mode of government near fourteen hundred years. Moreover the patron saint who founded it, and from whom it takes its name, deserves this poetical record, as he is, perhaps, the only saint that ever contributed to the establishment of freedom.

> " Nor e'er her former pride relate
> To sad Liguria's bleeding state."

In these lines the poet alludes to those ravages in the state of Genoa, occasioned by the unhappy divisions of the Guelphs and Gibelines.

> "—— When the favour'd of thy choice,
> The daring archer heard thy voice."

14

For an account of the celebrated event referred
to in these verses, see Voltaire's Epistle to the
King of Prussia.

> " Those whom the rod of Alva bruised,
> Whose crown a British queen refused ! "

The Flemings were so dreadfully oppressed by
this sanguinary general of Philip the Second, that
they offered their sovereignty to Elizabeth; but,
happily for her subjects, she had policy and mag-
nanimity enough to refuse it. Desormeaux, in
his Abrégé Chronologique de l'Histoire d'Espagne,
thus describes the sufferings of the Flemings:
" Le duc d'Albe achevoit de réduire les Flamands
au désespoir. Après avoir inondé les échafauds
du sang le plus noble et le plus précieux, il fai-
soit construire des citadelles en divers endroits,
et vouloit établir l'Alcavala, ce tribute onéreux
qui avoit été longtems en usage parmi les Espa-
gnols." — *Abrég. Chron. tom. iv.*

> " ——— Mona,
> Where thousand elfin shapes abide."

Mona is properly the Roman name of the Isle of
Anglesey, anciently so famous for its Druids;
but sometimes, as in this place, it is given to the
Isle of Man. Both these isles still retain much
of the genius of superstition, and are now the
only places where there is the least chance of
finding a fairy.

ODE TO A LADY,

ON THE DEATH OF COLONEL ROSS, IN THE ACTION OF
FONTENOY.

THE iambic kind of numbers in which this ode
is conceived seems as well calculated for tender
and plaintive subjects, as for those where strength
or rapidity is required. — This, perhaps, is owing
to the repetition of the strain in the same stanza;
for sorrow rejects variety, and affects a uni-
formity of complaint. It is needless to observe,
that this ode is replete with harmony, spirit, and
pathos; and there surely appears no reason why
the seventh and eighth stanzas should be omitted
in that copy printed in Dodsley's Collection of
Poems.

ODE TO EVENING.

THE blank ode has for some time solicited admission into the English poetry; but its efforts, hitherto, seem to have been in vain, at least its reception has been no more than partial. It remains a question, then, whether there is not something in the nature of blank verse less adapted to the lyric than to the heroic measure, since, though it has been generally received in the latter, it is yet unadopted in the former. In order to discover this, we are to consider the different modes of these different species of poetry. That of the heroic is uniform; that of the lyric is various; and in these circumstances of uniformity and variety probably lies the cause why blank verse has been successful in the one, and unacceptable in the other. While it presented itself only in one form, it was familiarized to the ear by custom; but where it was obliged to assume the different shapes of the lyric muse, it seemed still a stranger of uncouth figure, was received rather with curiosity than pleasure, and entertained without that ease or satisfaction which acquaintance and familiarity produce. — Moreover, the heroic blank verse obtained a sanction of infinite importance to its general reception, when it was adopted by one of the greatest poets the world ever produced, and was made the vehicle of the noblest poem that ever was written. When this poem at length extorted that applause which ignorance and prejudice had united to withhold, the versification soon found its imitators, and became more generally successful than even in those countries from whence it was imported. But lyric blank verse had met with no such advantages ; for Mr. Collins, whose genius and judgment in harmony might have given it so powerful an effect, has left us but one specimen of it in the Ode to Evening.

In the choice of his measure he seems to have had in his eye Horace's Ode to Pyrrha ; for this ode bears the nearest resemblance to that mixed kind of the asclepiad and pherecratic verse ; and that resemblance in some degree reconciles us to the want of rhyme, while it reminds us of those great masters of antiquity, whose works had no need of this whimsical jingle of sounds.

From the following passage one might be induced to think that the poet had it in view to render his subject and his versification suitable to each other on this occasion, and that, when he addressed himself to the sober power of Evening,

he had thought proper to lay aside the foppery
of rhyme:

> " Now teach me, maid composed,
> To breathe some soften'd strain,
> Whose numbers, stealing through thy darkening vale,
> May not unseemly with its stillness suit,
> As, musing slow, I hail
> Thy genial loved return! "

But whatever were the numbers or the versifi-
cation of this ode, the imagery and enthusiasm it
contains could not fail of rendering it delightful.
No other of Mr. Collins's odes is more generally
characteristic of his genius. In one place we dis-
cover his passion for visionary beings:

> " For when thy folding-star arising shows
> His paly circlet, at his warning lamp
> The fragrant Hours, and Elves
> Who slept in buds the day,
>
> And many a Nymph who wreathes her brows with sedge,
> And sheds the freshening dew, and, lovelier still,
> The pensive Pleasures sweet,
> Prepare thy shadowy car."

In another we behold his strong bias to melan-
choly:

> " Then let me rove some wild and heathy scene,
> Or find some ruin 'midst its dreary dells,
> Whose walls more awful nod
> By thy religious gleams."

Then appears his taste for what is wildly grand and magnificent in nature; when, prevented by storms from enjoying his evening walk, he wishes for a situation,

> " That from the mountain's side
> Views wilds and swelling floods; "

And through the whole, his invariable attachment to the expression of painting :

> " —— and marks o'er all
> Thy dewy fingers draw
> The gradual dusky veil."

It might be a sufficient encomium on this beautiful ode to observe, that it has been particularly admired by a lady to whom nature has given the most perfect principles of taste. She has not even complained of the want of rhyme in it; a circumstance by no means unfavourable to the cause of lyric blank verse; for surely, if a fair reader can endure an ode without bells and chimes, the masculine genius may dispense with them.

THE MANNERS.

AN ODE.

FROM the subject and sentiments of this ode, it seems not improbable that the author wrote it about the time when he left the university; when, weary with the pursuit of academical studies, he no longer confined himself to the search of theoretical knowledge, but commenced the scholar of humanity, to study nature in her works, and man in society.

The following farewell to Science exhibits a very just as well as striking picture : for however exalted in theory the Platonic doctrines may appear, it is certain that Platonism and Pyrrhonism are nearly allied :

> " Farewell the porch, whose roof is seen,
> Arch'd with the enlivening olive's green:
> Where Science, prank'd in tissued vest,
> By Reason, Pride, and Fancy drest,
> Comes like a bride, so trim array'd,
> To wed with Doubt in Plato's shade ! "

When the mind goes in pursuit of visionary systems, it is not far from the regions of doubt ; and the greater its capacity to think abstractedly, to reason and refine, the more it will be exposed to, and bewildered in, uncertainty.—From an enthusiastic warmth of temper, indeed, we may for a while be encouraged to persist in some favourite doctrine, or to adhere to some adopted system; but when that enthusiasm, which is founded on the vivacity of the passions, gradually cools and dies away with them, the opinions it supported drop from us, and we are thrown upon the inhospitable shore of doubt.—A striking proof of the necessity of some moral rule of wisdom and virtue, and some system of happiness established by unerring knowledge, and unlimited power.

In the poet's address to Humour in this ode there is one image of singular beauty and propriety. The ornaments in the hair of Wit are of such a nature, and disposed in such a manner, as to be perfectly symbolical and characteristic :

> " Me too amidst thy band admit,
> There where the young-eyed healthful Wit,
> (Whose jewels in his crisped hair
> Are placed each other's beams to share,
> Whom no delights from thee divide)
> In laughter loosed, attends thy side."

Nothing could be more expressive of wit, which consists in a happy collision of comparative and relative images, than this reciprocal reflection of light from the disposition of the jewels.

> " O Humour, thou whose name is known
> To Britain's favour'd isle alone."

The author could only mean to apply this to the time when he wrote, since other nations had produced works of great humour, as he himself acknowledges afterwards.

> " By old Miletus," &c.
> " By all you taught the Tuscan maids," &c.

The Milesian and Tuscan romances were by no means distinguished for humour; but as they were the models of that species of writing in which humour was afterwards employed, they are, probably for that reason only, mentioned here.

THE PASSIONS.

AN ODE FOR MUSIC.

IF the music which was composed for this ode had equal merit with the ode itself, it must have been the most excellent performance of the kind in which poetry and music have, in modern times, united. Other pieces of the same nature have derived their greatest reputation from the perfection of the music that accompanied them, having in themselves little more merit than that of an ordinary ballad : but in this we have the whole soul and power of poetry — expression that, even without the aid of music, strikes to the heart ; and imagery of power enough to transport the attention, without the forceful alliance of corresponding sounds! what, then, must have been the effect of these united!

It is very observable, that though the measure is the same, in which the musical efforts of Fear, Anger, and Despair are described, yet, by the variation of the cadence, the character and operation of each is strongly expressed: thus particularly of Despair:

> " With woful measures wan Despair —
>   Low, sullen sounds his grief beguiled,
> A solemn, strange, and mingled air,
>   'Twas sad by fits, by starts 'twas wild."

He must be a very unskilful composer who could not catch the power of imitative harmony from these lines !

The picture of Hope that follows this is beautiful almost beyond imitation. By the united powers of imagery and harmony, that delightful being is exhibited with all the charms and graces that pleasure and fancy have appropriated to her :

> Relegat, qui semel percurrit ;
>   Qui nunquam legit, legat.

> " But thou, O Hope, with eyes so fair,
>   What was thy delighted measure !
> Still it whisper'd promised pleasure,
>   And bade the lovely scenes at distance hail !
> Still would·her touch the strain prolong,
>   And from the rocks, the woods, the vale,
> She call'd on Echo still through all the song ;
>   And where her sweetest theme she chose,
>   A soft responsive voice was heard at every close,
> And Hope enchanted smiled, and waved her golden hair."

In what an exalted light does the above stanza

place this great master of poetical imagery and harmony! what varied sweetness of numbers! what delicacy of judgment and expression! how characteristically does Hope prolong her strain, repeat her soothing closes, call upon her associate Echo for the same purposes, and display every pleasing grace peculiar to her!

" And Hope enchanted smiled, and waved her golden hair."

Legat, qui nunquam legit ;
Qui semel percurrit, relegat.

The descriptions of Joy, Jealousy, and Revenge are excellent, though not equally so. Those of Melancholy and Cheerfulness are superior to every thing of the kind ; and, upon the whole, there may be very little hazard in asserting, that this is the finest ode in the English language.

AN EPISTLE

TO SIR THOMAS HANMER, ON HIS EDITION OF SHAKESPEARE'S WORKS.

THIS poem was written by our author at the university, about the time when Sir Thomas Hanmer's pompous edition of Shakespeare was printed at Oxford. If it has not so much merit as the rest of his poems, it has still more than the subject deserves. The versification is easy and genteel, and the allusions always poetical. The character of the poet Fletcher in particular is very justly drawn in this epistle.

DIRGE IN CYMBELINE.

ODE ON THE DEATH OF THOMSON.

MR. COLLINS had skill to complain. Of that mournful melody, and those tender images, which are the distinguishing excellencies of such pieces as bewail departed friendship, or beauty, he was an almost unequaled master. He knew perfectly to exhibit such circumstances, peculiar to the objects, as awaken the influences of pity; and while, from his own great sensibility, he felt what he wrote, he naturally addressed himself to the feelings of others.

To read such lines as the following, all-beautiful and tender as they are, without corresponding emotions of pity, is surely impossible:

> " The tender thought on thee shall dwell;
> Each lonely scene shall thee restore,
>   For thee the tear be duly shed;
> Beloved till life can charm no more,
>   And mourn'd till Pity's self be dead."

The Ode on the Death of Thomson seems to have

been written in an excursion to Richmond by water. The rural scenery has a proper effect in an ode to the memory of a poet, much of whose merit lay in descriptions of the same kind; and the appellations of " Druid," and "meek Nature's child," are happily characteristic. For the better understanding of this ode. it is necessary to remember, that Mr. Thomson lies buried in the church of Richmond.

THE END.

CPSIA information can be obtained
at www.ICGtesting.com
Printed in the USA
LVHW021552020421
683322LV00014B/638

9 781377 289922